VIDEO
MARKETING
RULES

HOW TO WIN IN
A WORLD GONE VIDEO!

LOU BORTONE

Video Marketing Rules!
Copyright © 2017 Lou Bortone

www.VideoMarketingRules.com

Printed in the United States of America
Book design: Carla Green, Clarity Designworks

ISBN-13: 978-1548286514

This book is dedicated to anyone and everyone who is courageous enough to share their knowledge and spread their message on video, especially those of us who don't like being on camera. This book is also dedicated to all the introverts, underdogs and camera shy entrepreneurs who feel the fear and do it anyway. You rule.

CONTENTS

PART 1: The 7 Stages of Video Marketing:

PART 2: The Practical Guide to Making Great Videos

Bonus Materials

ACKNOWLEDGMENTS

Big thanks to my Family, who give me the freedom and flexibility to do what I do. Thanks also to Peter Shankman and the entire Shankminds crew for always having my back. And, most of all, special thanks to my awesome clients and colleagues, along with the thousands of students who have taken my courses, purchased my products, attended my workshops and opened my emails. You make it worth all the effort!

FOREWORD

A World Gone Video

Forbes calls it "the premier communications tool of today;" Mark Zuckerberg says it's a "megatrend", and *The Guardian* heralds it as the "future of content marketing."

Of course, we're talking about online video, a tool so powerful and ubiquitous that it has come to dominate the media landscape.

Once the bastion of TV networks and media moguls, today social platforms like YouTube, Facebook, Instagram and Snapchat have put the power of video into the hands of the masses, making anyone with mobile phone an anytime, anywhere, worldwide broadcaster.

You'd have to go back centuries to the invention of the printing press in 1450, or to the rise of the Internet itself, to find a more tectonic cultural shift. The Revolution *is* being televised, but it's being created and broadcast by you and me.

And all that "user generated content" (500 hours of video uploaded to YouTube every single minute, at last count), is also being consumed anytime, anywhere and on any device. Online video has put us in the driver's seat, both as a producer and as a viewer.

Long gone are the days of NBC's *must-see TV* and "appointment viewing" *Seinfeld* Thursdays at 9 p.m. Now we binge watch *House of Cards* on Netflix, or fire up our Kindle to check out *Hand of God*, a series produced, not by Hollywood, but by Amazon.com.

But even more impressive than Netflix' 98.75 million streaming subscribers may be the fact that YouTube stars like PewDiePie have 56 million subscribers who have helped him rack up over 15 billion video views. (That's a bit better than the typical *Tonight Show* audience of

3.3 million). Meanwhile, YouTube make up artist Michelle Phan is reportedly pulling down over $441 million annually from her YouTube videos. Not too shabby!

And YouTube is not the only game in town when it comes to online video. Facebook is now generating 8 billion video views per day, and Snapchat is climbing fast with 6 billion views per day. These social platforms are well on their way to becoming video networks, with far more reach and influence than the traditional broadcast and cable networks.

All these statistics and success stories simply prove what we've suspected since the advent of the iPhone: We're living in what my colleague Lou Bortone calls "a world gone video." That means if you're running a business — any kind of business — you need to "go video," too.

If you're not creating video for your business, start. If you're already doing video, do more. Do better. This book will show you how. The opportunity has never been greater...

—**Peter Shankman**, Author, *Zombie Loyalists,*
Nice Companies Finish First, and *Faster Than Normal*

INTRODUCTION

Welcome to the
Online Video Revolution!

The Web – and in fact the whole world – has gone video. Cisco Systems predicts that, in the next couple of years, 90% of all web traffic will be video. Video has become the way we share, the way we communicate, the way we connect, and the way we buy and sell.

Video has also become the way we search (YouTube is the second most popular search engine), the way we "surf," and the way we make buying decisions. 65% of consumers will visit a brand's website and make a purchase decision after watching a video.

As an online entrepreneur, video marketing is your single most powerful tool for getting more visibility more quickly, so you can get your message out, attract your ideal clients, make more money and have more impact. It's no surprise that ReelSEO reports 87% of online marketers are now using video to promote their products and services. And eMarketer confirms that 4 times as many consumers would rather watch a video about a product than read about it.

Want more proof that the world's gone video? It's also reported that your chances of getting a page one listing on Google search increase by 53 times when you use video. You can also experience a dramatic 46% more conversion lift with video. But perhaps most telling and most important for anyone doing business online is the Aberdeen Group's research that shows that businesses using video grow revenue 49% faster than those who don't use video.

Video increases your visibility and credibility, it boosts your search engine rankings, and it rapidly accelerates the sales process. Video is clearly a more personal and familiar medium, and one that can truly create a strong and lasting relationship with your customers.

Video marketing is relationship marketing — crucial for connecting, building loyalty and developing the "know, like and trust" factor which is so important when doing business online. And if you're doing any kind of business online, there's nothing better than hearing "I feel like I already know you," from new people or prospects who you meet offline, in the "real" world. Video creates that "I feel like I already know you" effect better than any other medium.

VIDEO STATISTICS

- 89 Million people in the U.S. are going to watch 1.2 Billion online videos today. (ComScore)
- Social video generates 1200% more shares than text and images combined.
- Video on landing pages can increase conversions by 80% or more.
- Businesses using video grow revenue 49% faster than those who don't use video. (Aberdeen)
- Video drives 157% increase in organic traffic from search engines.
- 4X as many consumers would rather watch a video about a product than read about it. (eMarketer)
- Every day, Americans watch more than 8,000 years worth of video on YouTube!

What's Inside?

This book, and the accompanying website, will walk you through everything you need to know to succeed with video marketing. Once armed with your new video "superpower," there will be nothing you can't accomplish using video marketing:

- Increase visibility and awareness for my business? Check.
- Build my brand online? Check.

- Drive more traffic to my website? Done.
- Improve my SEO and Google rankings? Got it!
- Attract new clients and generate more revenue? Yup!

Marketing with video will help you do all this and more. It's the ultimate secret weapon in your marketing arsenal.

To get you there as quickly as possible, this book is divided into two parts:

Part I covers the 7 key stages of video marketing, including Purpose, Premise, Production, Platforms, Promotion, Power and Profit. These are the pillars of video marketing and they create the foundation for a powerful and sustainable marketing and branding presence. The 7 stages are also what I teach my clients and students in my "Video Marketing Success System" online course and coaching program.

Part II of the book is designed as a practical guide and reference resource for the "nuts and bolts" of video creation. This is the "how to" section that you can use to master a specific skill or learn more about any aspect of video creation and distribution. You can read the entire book in order to become a true "video ninja," or skip around to the brief chapters in Part II to get up to speed on a certain element of the process.

Either way, you've got a comprehensive guide to mastering video marketing so you can build your brand and grow your business.

Needless to say, technology moves pretty fast and things in the online video space move even faster. Fortunately, most of the principles and strategies outlined in this book are evergreen and not "tech-dependent."

However, video software and platforms come and go quickly (anyone remember Blab or Meerkat?), so we've also got a "Video Marketing Rules" companion website to keep you up to date on the latest and greatest video innovations. You can find that at: www.VideoMarketingRules.com

One word to the wise in that regard: Don't get too enamored with any one, specific platform or app, as it may be gone tomorrow! Try to avoid getting hung up on the technology, because the only certainty is change. Bear in mind that, when all is said and done, video marketing is about connection and relationships, not technology and equipment.

Stick with the tried and true marketing principles outlined in this book and you'll be on your way!

VIDEO BENEFITS

1. Increase your awareness and visibility
2. Improve your SEO/Google rankings
3. Build a brand online
4. Be seen as the "go to" expert in your niche
5. Drive traffic to your website
6. Grow your mailing list and build a community
7. Get more clients!

The Three Golden Rules of Video Marketing

Since the dawn of YouTube, way back in the dark ages of 2005, online video has sought to educate, engage and empower people. These are essentially the three golden rules of video marketing: *Educate, engage and empower.*

Just about any video you create will fall into one (or more) of these three categories. A quick look at YouTube will reveal that most videos follow these three key tenets:

Educate: The sheer number of "how to" videos on YouTube validates that teaching, demonstrating and informing is a mainstay of online video. If your video sets our to teach or instruct, you're on the right track. Your "educational" video should inform, enlighten and even inspire your viewer. If your video is able to be the solution to someone's problem, or the answer to their challenge, you've done your job. Whether the ultimate goal of your video is to establish your credibility or to sell a product, you must add value in the process.

Engage: Great videos not only educate, but also engage or entertain the viewer. A video can educate, but still be painfully boring. Once you add engagement to the mix, then you're really on to something! Engaging videos connect, they pull the viewer in and capture their attention and imagination. Engaging videos create a relationship with the viewer, establishing

a powerful bond. Engaging videos fascinate and captivate —
they involve and enthrall your viewer. These are the videos
that get shared and spread. Of course, engaging videos also
entertain — clearly a key element of any successful video!

Empower: Videos that empower, enlighten or inspire your
viewers may be less common, but they are incredibly powerful. Empowering videos have the unique ability to enable your
viewer to make a change or open up new possibilities. Videos
that empower can also influence and motivate your viewer.
Empowering and inspiring videos may be the most difficult to
create, but the rewards can be awesome.

When your video meets one of the three golden rules of video marketing, you're on the path to success. If the video hits two or three of
the golden rules, then you've hit a video home run. So always swing
for the proverbial fences as you create your video, and endeavor to
educate, engage and/or empower.

As we go through the 7 Stages of Video Marketing, keep the three
golden rules of "Educate, Engage, Empower" in mind and let the three
axioms guide your efforts. Think of them as the "holy trinity" of online
video as you create your content and share your messages via video.

With that in mind, let's dive into the first crucial element of video
marketing: Your video's goal or purpose.

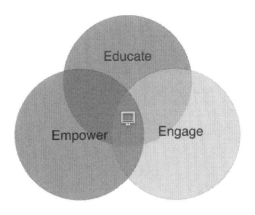

PART 1

The 7 Stages of Video Marketing:
The Video Marketing Success System

There are 7 stages that make up the Video Marketing Success System. They are:

- Stage 1 — **Video Purpose** — Establishing your video goals and objectives

- Stage 2 — **Video Premise** — Developing your video content and messaging

- Stage 3 — **Video Production** — Determining your equipment and technical needs

- Stage 4 — **Video Platforms** — Finding your video "Sweet Spot" and style

- Stage 5 — **Video Promotion** — Sharing and distributing your video for maximum reach

- Stage 6 — **Video Power** — Leveraging and repurposing your videos for increasing visibility

- Stage 7 — **Video Profit** — Monetizing your videos through video product creation and sales

I developed these 7 keys to video success based on over 10 years of video marketing experience with hundreds of clients and thousands of videos. We've seen what works in the real world and what it takes to create great videos that get results and return on investment.

We've found over and over again, in any industry and any niche, that this process, in this order, works best. It's the quickest, easiest and most effective route to consistent video success. So follow this 7 part process, step-by-step, and you'll master video marketing in short order!

THE 7 STAGES OF VIDEO MARKETING SUCCESS

- Purpose: What is the GOAL of your video?
- Premise: What is the MESSAGE of your video?
- Production: How will you CREATE your video?
- Platform: What TYPE of video will you create?
- Promotion: How will you DISTRIBUTE your video?
- Power: How will you LEVERAGE your video?
- Profit: How will you MONETIZE your video?

Video Purpose: Establishing Your Video Goals and Objectives

Strategy First

You may be surprised to learn that video marketing, or at least successful video marketing, is not about which camera to use, what's the best microphone, or even lighting and editing. That's production, not marketing.

To be effective with video, the emphasis needs to be on your marketing strategy. You must ask: What is the goal of the video? What business objective will it accomplish? Who will be viewing the video, and what do you want the viewer to do after they watch it? These are just a few of the marketing questions that must be addressed before you ever set up a light or fire up the webcam.

Obviously, production is important (and we'll get to that), but it's still not marketing. Start with strategy and that will determine how much (or how little) equipment you need. So think strategy first, tools, equipment and technology later. Goals over gadgets, as I like to say!

Many video "newbies" make the mistake of stocking up on fancy equipment, high-end video cameras or expensive software. Once all their gear is finally in place, they often have a "now what?" (or more likely, "oh shit!") moment when they realize they've put the cart before the horse.

Thinking that equipment alone with help you produce great video is just like thinking that simply buying a treadmill or stair master will get you in shape. You still have to know how to use it and do the work!

Depending on your video marketing goals, you may not need a lot of equipment. It's more likely that you can get a great start just by using the video camera on your smartphone or the webcam on your laptop or tablet. Again, goals before tech.

Let's take Tania, for instance, a wellness coach who wants to build her online business and eventually sell wellness workshops and health-related products online. Tania's video goals include establishing her expertise in her niche and developing trust and credibility among her target-market of health-conscious boomers.

Because she needs to build her online visibility and credibility, Tania decides to create a video tips series to post on YouTube and her blog. Since content matters more than quality to her audience, Tania doesn't need to invest in high-end equipment. In fact, she can simply use the webcam on her computer to record her health tips, and then do some quick edits in iMovie (or even using YouTube's onboard editor). No big production is needed here — Just get those video tips posted quickly and consistently.

If Tania's goal was to get paid speaking gigs or appearances on TV news or talk shows, she may have taken a different approach and hired a professional camera crew to tape her segments. Production values would be more important for that more discerning audience. Let your strategy drive your technology requirements...

We'll do a much deeper dive into video production and equipment in Chapter 3, but if you've already got a good sense of your video goals and you simply can't wait to jump in, here are the essentials. All you really need to start creating videos is:

- A computer with good Internet access, or at the very least a smartphone that connects you to the web.

- Any kind of video camera, whether it's a webcam, smartphone, tablet, traditional cam corder, or whatever device you have available that records video.

- You should have a YouTube account, where you can upload and host your videos for free.

- You should also have a Facebook account, since Facebook has become so video-centric. This will also give you the ability to broadcast from your smartphone to Facebook Live.

- And perhaps most important, you'll also need commitment and persistence!

As you begin your journey into the world of video, your mantra should be "keep it simple!" The goal should always be to simplify and streamline the process so you can get your videos done and out to the world. Especially when you're just starting out, focus on content over quality!

That brings us back to step one: Video Purpose: Establishing Your Video Goals and Objectives.

The video process all starts with your marketing goals. There must be reason you're doing video, aside from the fact that everyone else is doing it! Recognizing that reason is the first step. What's your "why" when it comes to video? What do you want to accomplish?

- Are you looking to increase visibility and awareness for a product or service?

- Are you trying to establish and build a brand? Launching or updating a website?

- Do you need to grow your online presence or create a fan base?

- Are you promoting an event or a project or a new book?

- Trying to be "found" on the Internet and increase your Google search rankings?

- Or perhaps you simply need to drive traffic to your website and attract new clients?

Knowing your video "why" will clarify and simplify the entire video process.

When I work with my private consulting clients, we typically begin with a "Video IQ" assessment to determine where they are in terms of video and where they want to go. I've included that "Video IQ" worksheet here, and I suggest that you take a few moments to review and complete it.

This exercise will really help you hone in on your video goals so, once you do get to the nuts and bolts, the process will be much smoother, and the outcome will be far more powerful.

VIDEO MARKETING IQ ASSESSMENT

8. **What are your *long-term goals* for video? (Choose up to 3)**
   - Book new business/attract new clients
   - Create greater engagement and build a fan base or community
   - Build and grow your mailing list
   - Drive traffic to your website or sales page
   - Create a steady stream of qualified leads
   - Launch a new product, service or initiative
   - Fill your webinars and workshops (online or live events)
   - Create awareness and build a platform to sell books or promote products
   - Increase your visibility and online presence
   - Develop better customer engagement and connection/ customer service

9. **What are your *immediate* goals for video? (30-60 days)**
   - Increase online visibility and presence
   - Improve search engine rankings
   - Generate awareness for a product, service or event
   - Launch a new product or service (book, online course, seminar)
   - Increase leads and conversions

10. What is the *single biggest obstacle* to you not using video more effectively?

11. How will you know (or measure) your success for your video marketing goals?

12. Do you currently use YouTube as a marketing and promotion vehicle? (Check all that apply)
    - Do you upload strategically (using titles, descriptions and tags?)
    - Do you optimize for SEO?
    - Do you include a call to action in all your videos?
    - Do you use custom thumbnails?
    - Do you add end card graphics to your videos?
    - Do you add annotations to your videos for interactivity and engagement?
    - Do you leverage and share your videos to social media sites?
    - Are your videos as professional and high-quality as they should be?

13. Do you currently use video marketing for publicity, promotion and visibility? If so, how?
    - Regular (i.e. weekly) video webinars or virtual video workshops (GoToWebinar, Instant Teleseminar, Zoom or Webinar Jam)
    - Consistent use of LIVE video via Facebook Live, Instagram, Skype
    - Posting video tips or how to videos to YouTube, Vimeo, Facebook, etc.
    - Video blog posts or video podcast
    - Video Sales Letters or video landing pages

14. **Are you using video marketing in unique ways and with different platforms to support your marketing and business initiatives? (Please check all that apply)**
    - On-camera videos (Talking head, Facebook Live, etc)
    - Off-camera videos (Camtasia, screencasts, PowerPoint, etc)
    - Event simulcasts, webcasts, or live streams
    - On-camera interviews or video summits
    - Mobile video (Instagram, Periscope, Snapchat, Facebook Live)

15. **Do you have a video editorial calendar or an overall plan for how to use video to support your key initiatives?**

16. **Where do you feel you need the most help and support with video?**

17. **What's the one biggest problem or challenge you'd most like to solve with video?**

My hope is that, once you've completed this exercise, you'll not only have a much better idea of your overall video marketing objectives, but that you'll also see the tremendous *possibilities* available to you through the medium of video.

It's also important that you play to your strengths. As you go through the Video IQ Assessment, you may start to realize that you or your company may be drawn to certain types of videos. Go with that! Some people (and brands) are more suited to on camera videos, while others may want to create animated videos, webinars or other "off-camera" methods.

Don't force an unnatural style; find the right video platform and "video voice" and start there. You can explore other styles and experiment once you gain more confidence. In Chapter 4, we'll go into more detail on how to find your "Video Sweet Spot."

There's obviously a great deal you can do with video, but you must determine what you *should* do — and what you should do first, second, third, etc.

With that in mind, it may also be helpful to caution you on what you should *not* do! Video newbies and rookies often make the same common mistakes, and we want you to avoid those traps.

Rookie Mistakes: Six Video Marketing Missteps and How to Avoid Them

With so many businesses realizing that video marketing is the key communications tool of the future, business owners are falling over themselves to get onboard the video bandwagon.

Deciding to use this powerful visual resource to get your message out is smart. However, once entrepreneurs jump into the video waters, most soon realize that it's a tough swim. There are several common pitfalls most business owners experience as they begin their video marketing efforts. Fortunately, most of these rookie mistakes are easily corrected.

Here are the six video missteps that will sink you faster than you can say "lights, camera, action."

Mistake #1: Not Thinking Strategically

As mentioned earlier, when you decide to create a video, you've got to know your goals! Too many people dive head first into their video production without setting a specific business objective.

- What do you want THIS video to accomplish?

- How is the video tied to your business goals?

- What is the call to action at the end of the video?

I've seen many videos that left me scratching my head wondering, "what was the point?" Know your goals going in.

Mistake #2: Message *Mishigash*

Closely related to rookie mistake # 1 is not having a clear message in your video. What are you trying to communicate and how can you get that message across simply and succinctly? Your video should have one key message, and you should know (and tell your viewer) exactly what you want them to do.

Mistake #3: Tech Obsession

Too many video neophytes get tangled up in the technology. If you let the tech trip you up, you'll never get your video done. The truth is the equipment choices should be the least of your worries. It doesn't matter what camera you use! Even a webcam or an iPhone will suffice. Don't make it more complicated than it needs to be. Remember, *goals over gadgets!* When it comes to technology, chances are you are over-thinking it. Point. Shoot. Post. Repeat.

Mistake #4: Picking the Wrong Platform

There are dozens of ways to create great video, from traditional talking head videos to off-camera PowerPoint videos or animation. Don't get tied down to one perception or method of video. On-camera talking head videos are fine, but think outside the screen for other options that may be more appropriate for your personality or your message.

You can use www.Powtoon.com to produce your own animated video, or publish with www.Prezi.com to turn your slide show into a dynamic, engaging video.

Facebook Live has exploded in popularity and provides an instant way to connect and engage with your audience in real time.

There are numerous platforms available, so find the one that's best for your business. We'll go into much greater detail about some of the most popular platforms in later chapters.

Mistake #5: Selling Too Soon

Online video is an excellent sales tool, and you could argue that every video is somewhat promotional in nature — even if it's just building your visibility or credibility. But starting out with a sales pitch video can be short-sighted.

It's vital that you first establish trust, add value and build your likability factor. (Video is great for this!) In short, you've got to serve first and sell second. Once you've developed some goodwill with your videos, then you can ask for the sale.

Like any marketing tool, it's a process, and you don't want to pitch until you've had a chance to earn their trust.

Mistake #6: Post and Pray

The final rookie mistake is all too common. Newbies think once the video is done, their work is done. In truth, it's just beginning. Too many businesses adapt a "post and pray" strategy — which isn't really a strategy at all! They upload the video to YouTube or their own site and wait for the views to magically appear.

In this "Field of Dreams" scenario, if you upload it, they will *not* come. At least not until you effectively promote your new upload.

Post and Pray is not a marketing strategy — you have to create a mini marketing plan for each video and determine how you're going to get eyeballs to your video.

One easy and often overlooked tactic is to simply leverage your video and get it on to as many platforms as possible. Start with YouTube, but share your video to Facebook, Instagram, Twitter, LinkedIn, Pinterest and even Slideshare.net. More outlets means more views.

If you're guilty of any of these video marketing offenses, the good news is that they are all easily avoided. Steer clear of these six common video "fails" and you can go from video newbie to video ninja in no time!

Plan for Success

The best way to avoid these common video pitfalls is to simply have a plan! With a specific goal and plan for each video, you can simplify and streamline the process. While you may think that the structure and discipline of video planning limits your creativity, the opposite is true. Staying on point with your video goal will actually provide more freedom and flexibility.

As you develop a plan for each video you create, there are a few things to consider for keeping your video strategy from going off the rails. Here are a few suggestions to provide "video focus:"

- Always keep simplicity in mind: What is the shortest distance between you and a completed video?

- You are using video as a business marketing tool. Know your "why" before you fly!

- As we mentioned earlier, there are dozens of styles and platforms for video. What's the best option for you and your business?

- Always put your goals and strategy *before* your technology and equipment.

- There are both on-camera and off-camera solutions, so you must determine the best option for your unique situation.

Being crystal clear on your video goal before you begin will save you time and help you avoid the common "video overwhelm" trap. While you may be eager to dive in and start creating, prep time is going to save production time. At the same time, you may also need to steer clear of the perfectionism trap. In most cases, your mantra should be: "done is better than perfect!"

Unlike the wild, wild west, where you could "shoot first and ask questions later," making effective video requires you to ask questions first and shoot later! Here are few of the key questions you should ask to clarify your video goals:

- What do your want your video to accomplish?

- What type of video will help you reach this goal?

- How will you measure your video's success?

- Is this video part of an overall marketing campaign?

- What can this video do for you and your business?

- Where will it have the most impact on your business?

As you develop your "video vision," and your video marketing strategy, keep in mind that you want to build and integrate video into your overall marketing strategy. Video should support and enhance your company's larger marketing objectives. Video should not be an "add on" or a "one off;" it's got to be baked into the big picture.

That means you've got to decide where and when to use video to support your company's goals. Where does it make sense to integrate video to strengthen or accelerate your plans? How and where will video give you the biggest "bump?" In addition, you have to consider how to make video a *consistent* part of your strategy. As I like to tell my clients, *"One and done won't get it done!"*

I also recommend that my clients (and you) create a "Video Editorial Calendar." Similar to a blog editorial calendar or a social media calendar, a Video Editorial Calendar will enhance your bigger marketing plan and keep you on track.

You can start with your annual marketing calendar, then begin adding video to the marketing mix where and when appropriate. Plot out key initiatives, product launches, sales, campaigns and other priorities, and determine how video can support those activities.

Your Video Editorial Calendar will also help you build in time for video production, video distribution and video promotion. Think of it as an overlay to your master planning calendar. You can do this every 90 days so each quarter's video activities are planned in advance.

A Video Editorial Calendar will keep you on track and ahead of the curve when it comes to producing your videos. If you know, for instance, that you've got a new product launch or a big webinar to promote in March, you can work backwards and determine when you'll need to shoot and produce a promo video. Consider the old Ben Franklin adage that says, *"If you fail to plan, you plan to fail."*

Use the A.I.M. Method to Create Great Video

Another tactic for your video planning is to use what I call the AIM Method. This consists of three key questions you can ask before you create your video.

Oftentimes entrepreneurs are in such a rush to establish a presence on YouTube, Facebook, Instagram or the latest video site du jour, that they miss a huge piece of the puzzle. Many business owners are taking a "ready, fire, aim" approach to video marketing. Taking aim is the missing element in most video efforts, and if you skip the "aim" piece, you're likely to fail.

I see this time and time again in my work as a video marketing consultant. *"Why do you want to do video?"* I ask. The initial responses are often the same: *"Everyone else is doing video, and we don't want to be left behind,"* or *"We want our message to go viral."*

But let's be practical. If you want your video marketing to produce a return on investment, then you've first got to decide exactly what you want that video to accomplish for you. You need to know what your specific goals are before you write the first word of your script or fire up the webcam.

You would think that this "taking aim" method is painfully obvious, but there are thousands of videos in the YouTube graveyard that prove otherwise. In fact, the vast majority of YouTube videos never get more than 1,000 views. Think your video can top one million views on YouTube? Good luck, since TubeMogul reports that an infinitesimal 0.33% of videos ever get more than a million views.

If you're only goal is to upload a nice Valentine's Day video for your mom and you're happy with 6 views, then don't worry about your video goals and objectives. But if you want to produce a video that moves the dial for your business, then you've got to plan accordingly.

I've created the **A.I.M. Method** for creating videos that accomplish your business objectives. AIM stands for Audience, Intent, and Motivation:

A – Audience: *Who is your target market for this video?* Who are you trying to reach? Do you know the specific audience for your video? Where is the best place to reach that audience?

I – Intent: *What's the Intent of your video?* What do you want the viewer to do after they watch the video? Click the buy button? Opt-in to your mailing list? Share the video with others? What is your call to action? Is your call to action clear and compelling?

M – Motivation: *How are you going to move the viewer to action?* What's their motivation? How will you compel them to act? Is the incentive strong enough to justify the action? Are the benefits powerful and appealing enough?

When you follow the AIM Method, your other considerations for video will become much clearer: You'll be able to determine what type of video will serve you best (on-camera vs. off-camera); you'll know exactly what your message has to say; and you'll have a much better sense of the best delivery platforms for your video (i.e. YouTube, Facebook, LinkedIn, etc.)

Use the AIM sequence for success and your videos will be focused, engaging and on target. *Audience. Intent. Motivation.* Simply remember: *"Ready. AIM. Shoot!"*

How to Create a Video Plan That Works

For most entrepreneurs, the biggest challenge with online video is just getting started. For many small businesses, even those who have no problem cranking out content, creating video content can be daunting and intimidating.

And once you've got that first momentous video finished, you've only just begun. As I've said, "one and done" does not work when it comes to video marketing, so you need a process and you need a plan!

The key to a successful, ongoing video marketing strategy is to develop a video plan that supports your overall business objectives. In fact, it's not enough to just "do video," you've got to create videos as a means to an end. Your videos should be designed to help achieve specific business goals.

What do you want your video to accomplish? Are you doing video for the visibility and exposure? Are you trying to build credibility and establish yourself as an expert in your niche? Do you want to improve your search engine rankings? Or perhaps you're looking to video as a way to generate leads and sales for your business. Again, your goals will determine your video direction.

Be sure to set realistic goals that support your business. Specific video goals may include:

- Developing a video presence online

- Adding an opt-in or welcome video to home page

- Creating a "video tips" series on YouTube to establish credibility and expert status

- Building a promotional platform to sell books or information products

- Creating a sales video to launch a product

- Starting a weekly videoblog series to consistently deliver your content

- Creating tutorials or demos to sell as video product

Try not to think of video as an "add on" or an extra thing you have to do. Video can be integrated into your current marketing plans. Make a list of your regular marketing activities (i.e. email marketing, blogging, social media) and decide how adding video can enhance or improve those marketing tools.

That may mean turning blog posts into video blogs, doing a video version of your ezine, or just adding video to your email marketing efforts by sending video mail. (Two services for easy video mail include BombBomb.com and MailVu.com).

Once you've set your goals and determined how to integrate video into your existing marketing plans, you can get more specific by scheduling your video activities using your Video Editorial Calendar.

Once you've got all your ducks in a row with planning and scheduling, you just need to refine your video process. Obviously, the process will vary depending on the type of video you are producing, such as on-camera or off-camera. Either way, you've got to create a step-by-step system that you're comfortable with — and one that can be easily repeated as needed.

If you're doing a typical on camera "talking head" video, your process might consist of:

1. Scripting — Having an outline or script so you're ready with what to say

2. Appearance — Are you ready for your close-up?

3. Staging and setting — Finding an appropriate spot where you can shoot your video

4. Lighting — Making sure you've got adequate light

5. Audio — Testing your sound to ensure good audio quality

6. Camera — Testing your webcam or video camera to make sure the shot looks good

7. Recording — Getting the right take that you're happy with

8. Editing — Making edits and embellishments as needed

Again, your process can be as simple and streamlined as you want to make it. As long as it works for you, and you can repeat the process whenever you want, you'll be good to go!

As you can see, the best videos are actually created before your ever fire up the webcam. Planning your video is the key to a successful shoot. Taking the time to plan ahead will make it much easier to create your videos — and to crank out quality videos consistently.

By now, I hope you're completely convinced that video marketing can rock your world and transform your business. And you're no doubt eager to jump right in and start creating videos. Although you'll be a seasoned pro by the time you get through this book, I can certainly understand that you want to test the waters right away.

With that in mind, I've included the next brief section to give you a cheat sheet for getting a head start. (Hey, you're not off the hook for actually reviewing the following chapters to really learn this stuff, but a few shortcut tips won't hurt!)

Why Start With Video?
10 Tips for Getting Out of the Gate Fast

Video is the fastest (and yes, easiest) way to make a big impact with the least effort and cost. You don't need a big, expensive website; you don't need a finished product; and, contrary to what the so-called gurus say, you don't even need a list of potential buyers (yet!)

You can start with videos on YouTube and Facebook (both free), promote your own product or service, or even use PLR (public label rights) "done for you" products to sell as an affiliate.

Not only can you sell with video almost immediately, but you an also build your brand, awareness and online visibility at the same time. Video gives you the biggest bang for your buck and the most potential reach for the least investment.

Take my client Evelyn from Costa Rica. She used an iPhone, iMovie, and her YouTube account to create simple, low-tech, Costa Rica travel tips videos to promote her luxury rental property. The videos were simple and authentic, with no frills and no fancy equipment — just good content and a little initiative.

Fast forward a few months and Evelyn was putting herself (and her rental property) on the map! Today, Evelyn has over a quarter million views on YouTube and has become the YouTube expert on Costa Rica travel. She now has individual videos with hundreds of thousands of views! Not bad for a once camera-shy technophobe!

When we worked with Evelyn, we emphasized content over quality to avoid getting bogged down by technology. Just get the videos done and posted to YouTube so they could be discovered. It worked like a charm for Evelyn, and the same approach can work for you!

Here are a few other keys for getting out of the gate fast:

1. Focus on your message first. Don't stress about the tech!

2. Just be yourself. Rehearse and be prepared, but don't change who you are!

3. Use as little equipment as possible such as your smart phone camera, webcam and YouTube.

4. Done is better than perfect!

5. Stick with uploading YouTube and Facebook first.

6. You can also post to your own website or blog.

7. YouTube is a beast with an enormous, built-in audience (and it's free!)

8. Find your "Video Sweet Spot." That's your ideal platform, whether on or off camera.

9. Share your video. Spread the word. Promote and repurpose it.

10. Rinse and repeat. Be consistent. Do a video series or produce several videos with a theme or topic.

That's all you really need to get going. Notice we didn't talk lighting, editing or fancy camera. None of that is needed at first as long as you've got good content. Just get started!

One important caveat: Notice that I said above that you've got to have good content to have good video. Content is still king and, without it, your finished before you can start. Your content is your message, and your message is the heart and soul and purpose of your video. What are you going to say, and how are you going to say it? That's the focus of Chapter 2, "Video Premise," where we show you how to develop your content and messaging for your videos. *Let's go!*

10 Compelling Reasons to Add Video to Your Marketing Mix Now

Online Video seems to be everywhere these days, and with good reason. Video works! Most experts agree that web video has become THE "must have" marketing tool for the survival of your business. And as if that's not reason enough, here are ten more compelling reasons why you need video — right here, right now!

1. **Google Loves Video!** And not just because they own YouTube. Video puts your SEO on steroids. With video, you can dramatically improve your search engine rankings.

2. **Video is Personal.** You can enhance your know, like and trust factor very quickly by appearing on video. Let your customers get to know you by seeing and hearing you!

3. **Video is Immediate.** Got an idea or a message? Got a webcam? Then you can make a video instantly and be online in minutes. Pull out your smartphone anytime, anywhere, and broadcast live to the world, on the fly and in the moment!

4. **Video Connects**. Nothing establishes a better connection with your clients and customers than video. Video creates that immediate bond. Video is engaging and captivating. Use it to bond with your customers, colleagues and prospects.

5. **Video is Growing Fast.** Video is way past the trend stage and has become a mainstream marketing tool. The Internet today is driven by video, so the sooner you get up to speed with this valuable resource, the better!

6. **Video is (mostly) Free!** With a free account on YouTube and a webcam or smartphone, you're good to go with online video. Facebook, Instagram and dozens of video apps are easily accessible at no cost.

7. **Video gives you worldwide exposure, 24/7**. Having videos online increases your visibility across the globe. Let your video work for you while you sleep!

8. **YouTube Rocks!** With an audience of a gazillion viewers, YouTube is *the* place to be seen online. Not only is YouTube now the 2nd most popular website on the Internet, and it's also the 2nd biggest search engine! Want a piece of the action? Create and upload your video to YouTube!

9. **It's Easier Than You Think!** iPhones, iPads, smartphones and even tablets make it easier than ever to capture and upload video. Most of these cameras let you upload directly to YouTube.

10. **Video Accelerates the Sales Process!** The best news of all about adding video to your marketing mix is that it greatly accelerates the sales process. People buy from someone they know, like and trust – and video can rapidly speed up that process. That means more customers, more quickly, and more coins in your pocket!

CHAPTER 1 VIDEO KEYS

1. Successful video marketing is made up of 7 key steps or stages.

2. All effective video starts by determining the goal and purpose of the video.

3. While technology is important, you must focus on goals over gadgets.

4. Video comes in many styles and platforms. You may need to change the way you think about video. Be open to all formats and solutions.

5. Use the Video IQ Assessment to determine your strengths and weaknesses.

6. Be strategic, but don't overthink it. In most cases, done is better than perfect.

7. Keep the process as simple and streamlined as possible

8. Utilize the A.I.M. (Audience, Intent, Motivation) Method to design your videos.

9. Integrate video into your overall marketing strategy. It should not be an after thought.

10. Be consistent. Create a Video Editorial Calendar to keep you on track and on target.

Video Premise: Developing Your Video Content and Messaging

Good News!

In Chapter 1, we discovered the importance of determining our "Video Purpose." Even with the emphasis on planning and strategy, the good news is that it is actually easier than ever to create great video. In fact, planning makes production faster and simpler.

We also know that there are hundreds of ways to approach video, along with new tools, software and apps that make video creation incredibly quick and easy. (We'll be revealing many of these tools in coming chapters).

To make video matters even better, you do not need a lot of equipment, and you can start right where you are, regardless of your experience level. You can use "everyday" technology like your smart phone to produce video anytime, anywhere. In most cases, content is more important than quality, so there are no excuses!

But despite the simplicity of video, the availability of technology, and the easy access to affordable equipment and platforms, the fact remains that you've got to have something to say! Your content is key, and your message matters.

What to say and how to say it on video is the focus of this chapter on determining your "Video Premise."

Your Video Vision

Your video's premise is the primary message of your video. But from a more global perspective, your premise is also your overall video "vision." Ideally, each of your videos should be part of a bigger, overarching theme or vision. Think of each video as a building block for your brand.

Your video vision includes the tone and feel of your videos, so that they reflect your voice and your style. In addition, your video vision encompasses what specific videos you'll create, including your "must have" videos that we'll discuss later in this chapter. So your vision is not only what you'll say, but how you say it. It's the content of your content!

As you develop your video content and messaging, think of your video as a visual story. After all, your videos really are just visual stories told with "moving pictures." That's why it's so important to integrate classic storytelling elements into your videos.

Tell Me a Story

Using storytelling principles in your videos will make them far more engaging and captivating. Integrating storytelling is vital, as stories are what will make your videos more memorable and "sticky." You've probably heard the old adage that "data tells, but stories sell." In fact, people remember stories over stats by a whopping 63% to 5%.

Stories are able to cut through the online noise and marketing clutter, and they draw your viewer into your world. Stories allow people to relate to you on a more personal level, even if they've never met you in person. And "Fast Company" magazine recently called storytelling the "biggest business skill of the next five years."

The power of storytelling in your videos cannot be understated, as stories elicit emotion and play an important role in persuasion. Stories actually engage many areas of the brain, and our brains process images 60 times faster than words! People much prefer stories over facts and actually retain information better with a story than with straight facts.

Like any good story, your video should have a beginning, middle and end, even if it's a brief, 20 or 30 second video. TV and radio commercials have been telling stories in quick, 15-second ads for decades, so brevity is no excuse for not using storytelling elements!

When telling your video "story," always include a clear call to action at the end of every video. You should get practiced at asking your viewer for something specific in your closing call to action, whether it's to call, click, comment, like, share, or visit your website.

If you're doing an on-camera or traditional "talking head" video, how you say it is just as important as what you say. Unless you're playing a character, you should speak naturally and talk the same way your normally talk! Use words you'd normally use in a conversation and avoid stilted language or industry jargon.

In most cases, your talking head video should feel intimate — like you're sitting across the table having a cup of coffee together with your viewer. Be relatable and seek to share an experience. And even though you may be speaking to a large audience via video, you should still talk as if you're talking directly to one viewer. Avoid language like, "hey, everyone," or "all you watching out there." Keep it personal and familiar.

Use the AIDA Method

If you're not sure where to start with your script writing, you can always go back to the tried and true A.I.D.A. method. AIDA is an acronym for Attention, Interest, Desire and Action. The AIDA model is well known in marketing and advertising circles, and is said to have been used in advertising as far back as the late 1800's.

The traditional advertising process involves the four stages a consumer moves through when making a purchase decision: Attention, or awareness, is when the consumer — or, in our case, the video viewer — becomes aware of a product or service. Interest is the stage where the consumer becomes engaged and interested in the brand or product. The consumer then develops a want or need for the product. And finally, action is the stage when the consumer becomes the buyer and makes a purchase decision.

This same AIDA advertising process can be used in video script writing, since your video is typically persuading your viewer to take some kind of action or possibly a purchase decision. The beginning of your video script must grab the attention of the viewer, ideally in the first few seconds. Once you've gained the viewer's attention, your video script has to spark interest and keep the viewer engage. Next, your video must create demand and arouse desire around your subject. And finally, your video script has to move the viewer to take action — which is why we insist that every video include a compelling call to action.

Keep the following structure in mind as you develop your video script:

- **Attention:** Begin by getting the attention of the viewer.

- **Interest:** Discuss what could be happening for them that they would need a product or service like yours. Emphasize a problem they have.

- **Desire:** Share your solution and explain why it's unique, special, different, and will solve their problem.

- **Action:** Be specific about how to contact you, how to buy, and what should happen next.

10 Key Online Video Scripting Guidelines:

Creating a script for your online video is much different than writing a script for a presentation, speech or live appearance. Scripting for online video is also a much different animal than traditional television or movie scripting.

Writing a script for online video is more personal, and should be more engaging than a typical

"on stage" or "on screen" appearance. With online video, you're (mostly) initiating a close, one-on-on conversation. You've got to speak naturally and conversationally.

In addition, online video scripts are often going to be short and sweet. With online attention spans so limited, you have to be direct and to the point. Keep your script as brief as possible.

With all that in mind, here are some video scripting guidelines to keep you on track:

1. Rule #1: There are no rules.
At least, not in the traditional copywriting sense. Online video is a very personal medium, so don't follow the old rules from another genre. Make the script yours and don't be afraid to get away from conventional writing rules.

2. Know your goal.
What's the point of your video? What do you want the viewer to do? Every word should lead towards your goal.

3. Hook from the start.
You've only got a few seconds to capture your viewer's attention, so grab them from the get-go! Jump right in and get to the point.

4. Use "you" in the first few seconds and keep it personal.
Your viewers want to know what's in it for them, so use "you" right away and tell your viewer what you're going to do for them and why you deserve their valuable attention.

5. It's still a story!
Remember, even though your video should be short and sweet, you still have to tell a story. You can use the time-tested "problem/solution" storyline or other storytelling elements.

6. Speak your target market's language.
Use words and phrases your audience will understand and relate to. Avoid jargon, and never, ever talk "down" to your viewers.

7. Know your tone/Stay on brand.
Put your personality into your script and stay true to your brand promise. Don't be afraid to be emotional, funny or quirky — especially if that's who you are. Keep it real!

8. Talk like you speak.
Be conversational and real. You don't need your "radio" voice or some stilted language. Your script should real just like you talk in real life.

9. Practice makes perfect.
(But done is still better than perfect!) Rehearse, for sure. But don't go crazy and do 99 takes just to get it perfect. People aren't perfect, so practice and be prepared, but don't go overboard.

10. Always include a strong call to action!
If you skip your call to action, you've wasted the entire video. You must state your call to action and tell your viewers exactly what you want them to do next, clearly and directly. Don't dance around the issue. Give your viewer guidance and get them to take action.

But What Do I Say?
I've been helping entrepreneurs and small business owners with video marketing since 2005, and even though video has become simpler and more mainstream, the number one question people ask is always the same: *What do I say on video?*

What to say and how to say it can be major obstacles to getting your video done and out to the world. If you're doing video, you've obviously got a message to deliver, a story to tell, or a product to sell. So start with that! "Begin with the end in mind," as goes the famous advice by Stephen Covey.

When crafting your script, you'll have to determine what message you need to deliver and what action your want your viewer to take. What do you want the viewer to do when the video is over? Be clear, concise and direct with your message's call to action. Keep your AIDA structure in mind as you write your video script.

As far as weaving storytelling elements into your message, you can write around a theme, a common experience, a memory, or tie in current events or trends. Remember, people remember and respond to stories over stats, so don't just spew facts — bake in those story elements!

If you need a jumping off point for story ideas, you can look no further than your everyday life. What's in the news and headlines? What's happening in pop culture? Can you piggyback on current events, holidays, anniversaries, historic events, or even personal happenings?

You can talk about work, family, favorite memories, proudest moments or life lessons. Or you could tie in historical figures, books, destinations, vacations. Just about anything goes, as long as you tie your story to a reason for telling it, such as a lesson you want to share or a point you want to make.

Also consider that your *existing* content and intellectual property can be repurposed for video! You can take blog posts, articles you've written, classes you've taught, or podcasts you've recorded and turn that content into videos.

There's no shortage of video topic ideas, and thus no excuse not to know what to say on your video. In most cases, your video content is going to be driven by your goals and objectives. A "welcome" video on your website's home page is going to require a different script than a "how to" video for YouTube. The overall purpose of your specific video will ultimately dictate the content of your script.

Video Topics Guide

Here are several other ideas for video topics to consider:

- Expert Tips Series
- Your back story — Your "why" (About Me video)
- Personal message on home page (Welcome Video)
- Sales or opt-in/landing page videos
- Video interviews or video panel discussions
- Product launch videos, series
- Facebook Live or YouTube Live videos
- Instructional or how-to demos
- Product demos, "how to use" videos
- Editorial — Your take or "rant" (video blog post)
- Your topic "Top Ten" list
- Testimonial or book review
- Live Q & A "Ask the Expert"
- Video webinars and/or training videos
- Webinar "invite" videos
- Thank you videos (thanks for registering, buying)
- Video webcasts or live streaming video
- Video mini-courses or tutorials
- Personal video e-mail (v-mail) messages
- Customer/Client "onboarding" videos
- Speaker reel, "sizzle" reel (for speakers)
- Portfolio or sample reel (for photographers, artists, etc)
- Screen share or screencast demos
- Inspirational videos (quotes, photos)
- Photo montage videos
- Birthday greeting videos

The 5 Must-Have Videos for Your Business

Take a look at any predictions, trends or business forecasts about marketing and sales and they all agree that Video Marketing will continue to be bigger and more important than ever.

Whether you market your business with email, social media or paid Facebook ads, video has become THE single best way to get seen and get sales on the web. So if you do any kind of business online, video is no longer a luxury – it is a must!

The problem is, most small business owners – even otherwise successful, six-figure coaches — still struggle with getting video "right." A patchwork of half-assed videos posted inconsistently is not a video marketing strategy!

If you fall into this category, as do most entrepreneurs, then you're missing opportunities and leaving money on the table. (Not good!)

To get your video act together and claim your share of the online video gold rush, there are five key videos that you need to produce or update: Your home page video, a YouTube video series, a regular video "show," video emails, and your "about me" video.

Let's look at each video in more detail:

1. Upgrade Your Home Page Video for Better Conversions and List Growth

Your home page video is your "first impression" video and your best opportunity to introduce yourself and really connect with your web visitors. Since first impressions are lasting impressions, your welcome video better be great! Keep it short, punchy and professional. Make sure you "finish strong" with a clear and compelling call to action. More often than not, that CTA is an opt-in offer so you can grow your list and keep in touch with your new peeps.

2. Revitalize and Optimize Your YouTube Channel with a New Expert Tips Series

There are so many good reasons why you need to have a strong YouTube presence: YouTube is the second largest search engine with billions of visitors daily. The SEO benefits alone are tremendous, and your visibility potential is enormous. If you can't be found on You-Tube, you're missing a huge opportunity. With "how to" videos being the most popular, an "expert tips" series is your chance to dominate your niche as the "go to" expert. Once you've created content-rich videos for YouTube, you've still got to optimize those videos with search-friendly titles, keywords, thumbnails, annotations, and other optimization tactics.

3. Create a Regular, Live Streaming Video "Show" for Appointment Viewing

With the advent of free, mass-appeal, live video streaming services like Facebook Live Periscope and YouTube Live, having your own web TV channel is not just a reality, it's practically a requirement. You can "plant your flag" and build your brand by launching a weekly (or monthly) web TV show – whether it's a webinar format using Facebook Live, or an interview series on zoom.us, The key is to establish a "beach head" before the space gets any more crowded. When it comes to live streaming, you snooze, you lose!

4. Connect and Engage Your Prospects with a Video Email Campaign

One of the simplest, yet most effective videos you can create is video email. Vmail provides you with a very personal and direct way to connect with your prospects, colleagues and clients. Vmail breaks through the clutter and commands attention. There are several video email resources, and some are free. Check out MailVu.com or, for a more feature-rich (paid) option, look at BombBomb.com.

5. Tell Your Story with an "About Me" Video or "Highlight" Reel

The fifth and final "must have" type of video is your about me or highlight reel video. An "about" video is your opportunity to bring your bio to life and share your story. A video is far more compelling than the usual, printed bio. And if you're a speaker, you can turbo-charge your about video by making it a highlight or "sizzle" demo reel video. A professionally produced speaker reel is vital if you hope to get bigger and better paid speaking gigs.

The last important puzzle piece is that you must post, distribute and share these videos for maximum reach and visibility. Use every marketing tool at your disposal, including YouTube, social media, email, and even paid advertising on YouTube and/or Facebook.

Video Script Samples

Here are a few additional tips for crafting your video scripts, along with some "fill in the blanks" welcome video script templates:.

Two of the first (and easiest) videos you should create for your business are a "welcome" video and an "about me" video. A welcome video, as the name implies, is a short video on your home page we coming visitors to your website. An about video is similar, but is usually more of a personal "bio" video with additional details about your background and experience. Here is a sample outline for each:

WELCOME VIDEO OUTLINE

Purpose: To give your web visitors a positive first impression, introduce them to you, and offer them a brief message about what they can expect to find on your website. Be sure to end with a strong call to action!

- Open with a short, branded intro (such as a logo reveal or title card) if you have one

- Introduce yourself to your web visitors as if you're welcoming someone into your home

- Briefly tell them who you are, who you serve, and the key result people get from working with (or buying from) you – Focus on the benefit to the viewer – think, what's in it for them?

- Give them a very succinct overview of what they can expect to find on your website

- End with one, direct Call to Action, such as an offer for them to opt-in (sign up) to receive your free report, video series, checklist, or whatever it is you are offering as your opt-in freebie

ABOUT ME VIDEO OUTLINE:

Purpose: To give your web visitors additional details about your background, experience and special skills or talents that could benefit the viewer/visitor. This video can appear on your "About" page, but you can also use it on other platforms, i.e. YouTube, as well.

- If you have a branded video intro, start with that...

- Introduce yourself and thank the visitor for taking the time to visit your site

- Provide some basic background info about you, as it pertains to your prospect

- Remember to keep your focus on the viewer, who is always thinking "what's in it for me?" Even though this is an "about me" video, the truth is you still have to make it "about them!"

- Talk a bit about your target market, and how you help them. Focus on the solutions you provide and the benefits your clients or customers receive.

- Close with an invitation to learn more by giving your email address or a way for prospects to "continue the conversation."

WELCOME VIDEO SCRIPT TEMPLATE

HI, THIS IS _____ AND IN THE NEXT____ MINUTES, I'M GOING TO (tell, reveal, explain, demonstrate) SHOW YOU HOW TO _____(final outcome or key benefit). (Optional: Insert show open, graphics or animation here)

AS A _____ (your expertise), I'VE HELPED (your target marketing) DO/HAVE/BE (result your target market gets). THAT'S WHY I WANT TO HELP YOU _____ (go into a bit more retail about what you do for people — What is the ultimate benefit they can gain from working with you?) I CAN HELP YOU (benefit(s) SO YOU CAN (ultimate outcome)

Share a key tip here or give them a small taste of what you provide — offer some value here to enhance your credibility... HERE'S HOW YOU CAN_____
_____ (or HERE ARE 3 QUICK TIPS TO_
_____)

IF YOU'D LIKE TO FIND OUT MORE (tease other ben-efits you provide), (call or sign-up) JUST ENTER YOUR NAME AND EMAIL ADDRESS IN THE SPACE PROVIDED, AND I'LL SEND YOU (your freebie or offer)_____
_____ SIGN UP NOW, SO YOU CAN START (benefit of your freebie or give-away)_____ (Be sure to reiterate your call to action! Tell the viewer exactly what you want them to do next — whether it's to sign up on your email list, call you, email you, visit your store location, etc.) THANKS FOR WATCHING, AND I HOPE TO TALK WITH YOU SOON...

PRODUCT SALES VIDEO SCRIPT TEMPLATE:

Note: There are dozens of ways to tell the story of your product or service, but one of the most popular is the tried and true "problem/solution" formula. This translates well to video, because it gives you the opportunity to show your target market how YOU are the solution they are looking for. Here's a sample:

YOU NEED (outcome client desires), BUT GETTING (outcome) CAN BE A REAL HASSLE… (Obstacle #1) CAN BE CHALLENGING, (Obstacle #2) CAN MAKE IT NEARLY IMPOSSIBLE , AND SOMETIMES IT FEELS LIKE THE ENTIRE PROCESS IS SETTING YOU UP FOR FAILURE. WELL, FAILURE IS NOT AN OPTION, SO SAY HELLO TO (your company), a (describe your business) that (solution your company provides).

WHETHER YOU'RE A (primary target market) OR A (secondary target market), WE'RE HERE TO HELP! WE (solution or outcome you provide), SO YOU CAN (ultimate benefit your customer receives). AFTER ALL, EVERYONE DESERVES (value or benefit you provide) WITHOUT THE FEAR OF (frustration or obstacle your customer faces). (Call to action here!) CALL, EMAIL, OR CLICK THE LINK BELOW TO GET STARTED. TAKE THE FIRST STEP TODAY TOWARDS (solving the big problem your customer wants solved!)

EXPLAINER VIDEO/DID YOU KNOW? SAMPLE:

DID YOU KNOW (insert little known fact about your industry)? IN THE PAST, (your target market) WAS LIMITED TO (customer challenge or limitation), BUT NOW (your target) HAS TO (new challenges or responsibilities of your target) JUST TO STAY ONE STEP AHEAD OF THE COMPETITION. THAT'S NOT EASY, BUT (your company) CAN MAKE IT A WHOLE LOT EASIER. WE HAVE THE RESOURCES TO SUPPORT (your customer) INCLUDING (your unique feature) TO HELP YOU (benefit), AND (your feature), SO YOU CAN (customer benefit). WE UNDERSTAND THAT YOUR INDUSTRY IS MOVING QUICKLY, WHICH IS WHY WE'RE DEDICATED TO (what you do to help your clients win). WE TAKE CARE OF (problem your customer has) SO YOU NEVER HAVE TO WORRY ABOUT (problem) AGAIN. (Customer's industry) MAY BE CHANGING FAST, BUT (your company name) KEEPS YOU ON THE LEADING EDGE, SO YOU CAN (ultimate customer goal). (Call to action) TALK TO US TODAY, AND FIND OUT HOW YOU, TOO CAN (achieve the big client need or desire)!

Script Cheat Sheet — Using the AIDA formula...

- What are you going to talk about/Why should they listen

- Who you are and who you serve (target market)

- What you can do for them — What's the result you get?

- Why they want what you can provide — Ultimate benefit Small taste or sample of the value you provide.

- Call to action — What should they do next? Give the viewer specific directions for the next step...

Scripting Tips

Before we wrap up our discussion on your video premise and message, let's look at the nuts and bolts of video scripting:

Most videos you'll be creating, such as your welcome video, a video tips series, or sales videos, should be relatively short. This is both by design and necessity. People have extremely limited attention spans on the web, so you've got to deliver your message as efficiently as possible.

In fact, if you've got a lot of information to share, or your content requires more time to explain, you may want to break up those longer videos into shorter, bite-sized segments. The trends continue to favor videos that are short and sweet.

So how long should your video actually be? According to a recent report by *Vidyard*, the average length of a business video is 8 minutes. However, that figured is skewed high because of long-form video content like webinars.

The majority of videos (56%) are less than 2 minutes long, while almost three-quarters of all videos published in the last year are less than 4 minutes long, says the Vidyard study. (See the pretty chart below!)

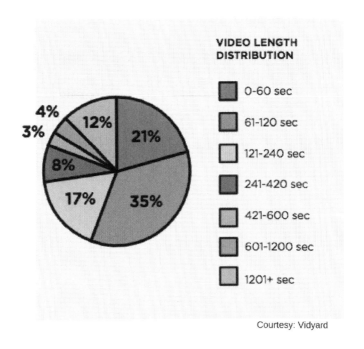

VIDEO LENGTH DISTRIBUTION

- 0-60 sec
- 61-120 sec
- 121-240 sec
- 241-420 sec
- 421-600 sec
- 601-1200 sec
- 1201+ sec

Courtesy: Vidyard

The real answer is less scientific: Your video should be no longer than it needs to be, since most of us have the attention span of a flea! I usually advise my video coaching clients to keep their videos under two minutes whenever possible.

Brevity also makes your job easier, as it's simpler to write and deliver a shorter script!

And while this entire chapter is devoted to script writing, that doesn't necessarily mean you have to script out your entire video, word for word. Ultimately, you have to find a messaging process that works for you, whether that's writing out your entire script, using a storyboard or outline, or simply writing out bullet points and ad-libbing your delivery.

Most beginners will likely want the security of a full script, but if you prefer a simple outline or bullet points, that's totally fine. You have to find what your most comfortable with, and whatever is going to feel most natural for you as you deliver your script — particularly if you're doing a traditional, on-camera video.

If you prefer working off an outline, be sure to include your key points and keep your AIDA structure in mind. One advantage of using an outline or bullet points is that you won't sound too stilted or look like you're reading. Obviously, the more familiar you are with your material, the more natural you'll sound.

Another great debate that comes up around the concept of script writing is whether or not to use a teleprompter. Again, this is going to be a personal decision based on your preferences. You may assume that using a prompter is easier, but it actually takes quite a bit of practice to read from a teleprompter. Sure, all the words are in front of you, but getting the timing right as the words scroll is an acquired skill.

I've had many clients who have used their laptop or iPad as a teleprompter (using software such as Teleprompt+), but in the end, many went back to using an outline and abandoning the prompter. Again, it takes practice to look as though you're not reading and your eyes are not going from left to right as you read the words off the screen.

Whether you're using a teleprompter or ad-libbing without a formal script, it's a good idea to at least memorize your script open and close, so you'll start and finish strong and confident. Of course, the best advice is simply to rehearse, rehearse, rehearse!

If you choose to write out your script, keep in mind that the average person speaks at about 140 words per minute. So if you want your final video to be under three minutes, your script target is just 420 words. And it's not just a matter of putting words on a page, because writing does not sound like speaking! As such, you have to "write for the camera," and make your written script as conversational and natural-sounding as possible.

Lastly, if whether you're using your webcam, iPhone, iPad or any other device as your camera, be sure to look at the camera lens, not the screen! This takes practice, and you have to be ever cognizant of where the camera lens is located on your recording device.

When all is said and done, you have to do what works for you. My own admittedly "low-tech" solution is often simply to put a post-it note on my computer screen with a 2 or 3 key bullet points! You'll find your own best practices, whether it's taping notes on the screen, using a full fledged script, or using a teleprompter.

Video Vision: Back to the Future

Another aspect of your Video Premise is your overall "video vision." What this really represents is looking at your videos not just from an individual video or script, but in terms of the big picture. As you develop your video scripts for your "must have" videos and other video projects, you must ask: where does each video fit into your grand scheme?

When you consider your bigger "video vision," think in terms of your master plan and overall business goals and objectives. With a video vision that supports your brand, you'll be able to better plan what to say in each video and how that supports the "big picture." Again, each individual video becomes a building block of your brand.

Earlier in this chapter we touched upon your "video vision," and we looked at your 5 "must have" videos, along with ideas for dozens of other types of videos and topics for your videos. Your video vision is where you get to put those puzzles pieces in place to see what makes the most sense for your specific business objectives. Your video priorities will be different based on your marketing goals. Someone who sells online courses is going to have a different video plan than an author who is releasing a new book every year or two.

Go back to your big picture business questions to develop your own video vision:

- How will you use video to support your business goals?

- How can you ensure that you'll use video consistently?

- Where do you want your business to be in a year?

- What are your key business initiatives for the year?

- Where and when will you use video to support your goals?

- How can video supplement and support your existing initiatives?

Once you've answered those broader video vision questions, you can then drill down to determine what you need for your individual videos by ask the following:

- What do your want your video to accomplish?

- What kind of video do you want to create?

- What do your want your video to accomplish?

- What is your key message?

- What do you want your viewer to do? (CTA)

- How will you get them to do it?

- Where will you distribute/promote/share your video?

- How will you follow up and plan your next steps?

Armed with your information about both your big picture goals and the individual videos you'll need to reach those goals, you can now create your customized Video Editorial Calendar. Your Video Calendar is where the rubber meets the road and you commit to specific dates for your video marketing initiatives.

When I work with my own video coaching clients, I recommend that they tackle this in quarterly increments. Creating a 90-day video marketing plan (using our Video Editorial Calendar) keeps us on track, without getting overwhelmed by the thought of planning out our videos for an entire year. (Though you can certainly try that if you're feeling ambitious!)

The Video Editorial Calendar is not created in a vacuum, but rather is built upon your existing marketing and business initiatives. Look at your key objectives for the next 90 days, and begin to determine where and how video can support those objectives.

Do you have a product launch planned that you can better promote with video?

What about a specific sale on a new product or service? (You'll need promo videos for that!)

Are you having a live or virtual event that will require video promotion support?

How about webinars, tele-seminars or summits that would benefit from video support?

Perhaps your rebranding or launching a new website. Again video will play a key role!

Once you've got your annual business plan and marketing initiatives in place, you can plot out your Video Editorial Calendar, indicating the dates and milestones where video will be needed.

Plan out your 90-day calendar, and be sure to include time for video production, editing, distribution, and all video-related activities. This will keep you on track and allow you the prep time needed to plug in your videos. When will you shoot the video? Put it in the Video Editorial Calendar. When will you post the video? Add it to the calendar!

Committing this to paper (or digital calendar) will keep you accountable and keep you on schedule and ahead of the curve when it comes to video marketing. And that's how video planning and video premise work together to make you successful!

Overcoming Videophobia

Of course, once you've got words on a page or bullet point on an outline, you've still got to *deliver* your script — particularly if it's a traditional, on-camera video. Writing the script is half the battle, but speaking your script and actually saying the words on camera is the next hurdle.

Performing on camera isn't necessarily a challenge for everyone, but for most folks it's not something they relish. If you're narrating your script over images or slides, it may be a bit less intimidating, but it's still an acquired skill.

Obviously, you can't do video marketing without doing video and, at some point, that's going to mean being on camera. Appearing in front of the camera can strike fear into the hearts of even the most seasoned entrepreneurs — a condition I describe as "videophobia."

Most of us suffer some level of videophobia, and precious few actually relish the thought of talking into a webcam or smartphone. After all, unless we're actors, news anchors, or Kardashians, being on camera isn't something we do every day. It's outside our comfort zone. It's not natural. In fact, it's not even like speaking from the stage. So, like any new skill, it has to be learned and practiced.

Ask 100 small business owners why they haven't yet used video to promote their products and services, and 95 of them will admit that it's fear of being on camera. Of course, if we break it down further, we hear common concerns such as "I don't like how I look on camera," or "I'm afraid I'll screw up and make a fool of myself." Shooting on-camera video is akin to public speaking, and we know how most folks feel about that!

While these are all legitimate fears, they are certainly not insurmountable obstacles. Granted, women have it harder than men to get "camera ready," but, believe me, us guys have our share of bad hair days and times when we're just not ready for prime time.

The surprising part of all this is that many entrepreneurs avoid the camera despite the fact that they understand the marketing power of online video. In fact, videophobia may be the only thing standing between you and the business success that video marketing provides.

So what should you do if you suffer from videophobia? Why should you miss out on the most powerful marketing tool available today?

Here are a few remedies to consider if you are one of the many business owners afflicted with videophobia:

1. **Practice, Practice, Practice.** – As the saying goes, all things are difficult before they are easy. But with time, patience and persistence, video does get easier. It's often a matter of trial and error, so put in the time to practice and rehearse. Even the highest paid movie stars do a dozen takes to get a scene right, so why shouldn't you? The more familiar you are with your script and the more you actually recite it out loud, the better it will be. There's simply no substitute for practice. Rehearse. Retake. Repeat.

2. **Get Creative. Get Crazy. Get in Character.** – Despite my 20 plus years in the television business, I was terrified of being on camera when I first started doing online video. I had always been on the other side of the camera, so suddenly being the center of attention was scary. One solution was to hide behind costumes and characters. I put my kids in my videos, my pets or props – anything to take the focus off me! Ironically, this worked like a charm and I became known for my wacky "LouTube" videos and crazy characters like Director Cecil B. DeMoron. It's a great way to lose yourself in the process and

conquer your nerves. Creating characters, personas or alter-egos can be fun and liberating! Think outside the screen and see what you come up with.

3. **Face Your Fear Head On.** – There's always the philosophy of "feel the fear and do it anyway," and "action cures fear." There comes a time when you just have to suck it up and do it. You may have to get outside your comfort zone to be on camera, but the end result is well worth it. Your initial efforts may be trying, but simply forging ahead and tackling the task will make you a better on camera "performer." The more you do it, the easier it will become.

4. **Do an Interview.** – This trick works wonders, because it's always easier to do video when there are two people involved. When it comes to video, two heads are easier than one. Having a partner or co-host takes a lot of the pressure off you, and can make the entire process more enjoyable. Facebook Live, Zoom, or even Skype make it easy to do video interviews or "two-shots," even if you and your co-star are on different continents. Interviews or panel discussions with two or more guests on camera can also take some of the focus (and fear) away from you. Enlist a friend or colleague and have some fun with it.

5. **Relax and Be Yourself.** – You do not have to be a celebrity or reality TV star to be on camera. YouTube and other mainstream video platforms have made it possible for anyone, anywhere, anytime to be on screen. People are watching videos to be entertained or educated. In many cases, they are looking to solve a particular problem. That means that it's your content that counts. Focus on your message. Share your story. Put your personality into your video, whether you're a gregarious extrovert or a card-carrying introvert. Be yourself and do what comes naturally.

Of course, being on camera is not the only way to create great video. Even off-camera videos can be effective. Still, for making a connection and establishing that all-important "know, like and trust" factor, there's nothing more powerful than appearing on screen.

So next we're going to talk about what it takes to appear on screen, as we delve into the ins and outs of video production! Armed with your Video Purpose, and your Video Premise, you're now ready for Video Production!

CHAPTER 2 VIDEO KEYS

1. Start with your "Video Vision" when crafting your video premise

2. Use classic storytelling principles in your script writing

3. Employ the AIDA (Attention-Interest-Desire-Action) method for writing

4. Know what to say — Review the "video topics' suggestions

5. Start with your "5 Must-Have" videos

6. Use the video script templates provided

7. Create and follow a Video Editorial Calendar

8. Practice to reduce any "Videophobia" you may experience

3

Video Production: Determining Your Equipment and Technical Needs

If you jumped right to this chapter first, I appreciate your enthusiasm and applaud your initiative. However, even if you did want to dive right in and start making videos, I'd encourage you to go back to the start and read the first two chapters so you'll know about your Video Purpose and Video Premise, before you attempt Video Production!

Once you've got that all important video foundation (Purpose and Premise) under you, you're good to go on the production side. This is the real nuts and bolts of video, and where concept becomes completion. This is where it's finally okay to ask *"What camera should I use?"*

So where to begin?

For that, we have to go back to the famous Stephen Covey quote, "Begin with the end in mind." Once again, your equipment needs will largely be dictated by what you want to end up with. Are you shooting an on-camera/talking head video, or an animated video? Are you narrating over slides in a PowerPoint video or recording your computer screen for a screencast video? You'll need different tools for different videos.

Keep in mind that your use of equipment or software will be based on your video goals and objectives (from Stage One: Video Purpose). I always encourage my clients and students to start with a "less is more" approach to video production. Don't add any equipment or complexity to your project that doesn't effect the final outcome. You've also got to determine if you're creating an off-camera, or an on-camera video.

There's no need to run out and start buying all kinds of equipment or software until you're absolutely sure you're going to need it! I hate to admit it, but I've got video equipment that I bought months ago, and I've never even taken it out of the box! While I couldn't resist the allure of the "bright, shiny object," I simply haven't had a need for it thus far.

Buying equipment for video is not the same as creating video. For example, buying a treadmill or ab roller may make you feel good about trying to get in shape, it doesn't guarantee that you'll exercise! (As evidenced by the treadmill gathering dust in my basement!) So hold off on the fancy lights, cameras or software until you've got a video plan in place.

Not to worry, we'll have plenty of equipment recommendations and ideas for you in the coming pages, but let's first focus on the production process so you can approach your equipment needs strategically.

The Production Process

The process of creating online video is not unlike the traditional film-making or television production process, though the online video system can be much simpler. The three phases of production include pre-production, production and post-production.

Pre-production, as the name implies, is everything that happens before you hit record. That includes planning, scripting, storyboarding, and all the elements of preparing for your shoot.

Production, of course, is the recording of the video, or the actual "shoot," as it's often called. And post-production, is everything that happens after the video is recorded, such as editing, adding music, graphics, etc. Let's take a closer look at each phase.

Pre-Production:

The video making process begins with pre-production and the idea or concept for your video. This includes all of the planning and development of your concept; writing the script or plotting out your story-board if you decide to go that route; your location scouting if you're shooting on location; and your equipment or software prep. (More on that soon).

From a practical standpoint, let's assume you're creating a talking head, on-camera video. You've decided that the "idea" of your video is to offer your best tip in a short video to be uploaded to YouTube. (Perhaps your goal is to increase your visibility and begin to establish credibility by sharing an expert tips series to YouTube or your blog). You've got your topic, so now you can work on your script. For a simple, 1-minute "tip" video, you won't need a storyboard or even an elaborate script. You can probably get away with an outline of your key talking points.

Next, you'll have to decide if you want to be on camera for the entire length of the video, or if you'd like to share your computer screen to show a slide or graphic.

Tip: I like to use zoom.us to record my tips videos, so I can appear on camera initially, then toggle to "share screen" on Zoom so I can show a slide or related image, then switch back to me on camera for the end of the video and the call to action.

You'll also need to determine your location and setting, or whether you'll record from your desktop using a webcam, or from your smart phone or mobile device. You'll have more control over the environment and background if you stick with a webcam from your computer.

Your equipment needs for an on camera tips video are simple: You'll likely opt for your webcam as your camera and microphone and record directly from your desktop or laptop. Again, your recording software can be almost anything — Zoom, Skype, Quicktime, iMovie, YouTube, Facebook — any application or software that will capture your recording.

You can use the microphone that's part of your webcam or, better yet, use an external USB microphone like the Blue "Snowball" or "Yeti" microphones. If you're recording from your smartphone, you can use the mic on the phone as long as you don't get more than an arm's length away from the device.

Now you know what you're going to say (using your script or outline), you've got your camera and recording app, and your "location" is set. It's time to hit "record" and move into the production phase!

Production:

Here's where we record your footage and do the video shoot itself. Hitting that "record" button is the single most powerful and important step in the process because, without that, we don't have a video!

If you consider production the stage where you create all the pieces for the final product, then you can include recording the video itself, as well as sourcing graphics or images for the shoot; recording voice-overs; and choosing background music or sound effects, as needed.

Going back to my "tips" video example above, our production would require a slide, screen shot or graphic in addition to my on-camera appearance. I might also select the background music I'm going to use for the video — or I could source the music later when I'm editing in post-production. Consider any graphics, lower thirds or other images you might need for your final product, but the main thing is to get your recording down.

Once you've captured your footage and you've got a "take" that you're happy with, you can move on to the post-production phase.

Post Production:

You may have heard the TV/film expression: "We'll fix it in post." This is a popular phrase in the industry, because there's a lot you can fix or improve in post-production. Thus, post is where everything comes together to finish the final video.

Post Production includes anything and everything that happens after the "shoot," primarily video editing, but also encoding or " rendering" of your video and, of course, sharing it with the world.

Editing can include everything from trimming or cutting the video clips; adding transitions or effects; adding graphics, titles, or lower thirds; adding music or sound effects; and adding any other special effects to embellish the video.

Video editing can be a source of stress or fear, because it can get complicated and require certain skills and software. However, most editing is optional, and many videos (such as Facebook Live videos) require little or no editing at all.

In our video tips example, minimal editing would be needed, other than perhaps cleaning up or "trimming" the video clips to ensure a clean start and finish, and possibly adding background music or a soundtrack "under" the vocal track. You've also got the option of adding a lower third identifyer or other graphics but, again, these are optional.

Many entrepreneurs are intimidated by the prospect of video editing because there is a learning curve involved. However, you don't necessarily need high end video editing software like Final Cut Pro or Adobe Premier to edit video. It's possible to do basic video editing right within YouTube, using YouTube's more than adequate on-board editor.

Another video editing option is to use online software such as WeVideo.com, a user friendly editing website that's "platform-neutral," meaning it works whether you're using a Mac or a PC. Other editing programs include iMovie, Sony Vegas, Cyberlink's Power Director, or Camtasia. (I'm on a Mac and have been using Final Cut Pro for the last 15 years!)

Try to find and use the video editing platform that's going to be easiest to use without having to become an expert video editor. If you prefer not to tackle the post production editing yourself, you can always outsource the task to a freelancer or video editor you can usually find on Elance or fiverr.com.

The goal, as always, is to keep it simple and find the most direct route between you and a finished video product. Fortunately, even a little editing goes a long way to making your video look more professional. Keep in mind that done is often better than perfect!

Producing an On-Camera Video

Now that we better understand the production process, let's take a closer look at the most traditional (and most useful) form of video:

The "talking head" (on-camera) video. The tried and true, "head and shoulders" shot is the bedrock of the video world. In many ways, there's nothing easier that firing up the camera and talking. (Although the prospect of appearing on camera may terrify some, it is now easier than it's ever been to do a talking head video!)

For your typical on-camera video, you simply need your video recording device and a microphone. In most cases, if you're using a webcam or a smartphone, both audio and video will be in the same unit. Depending on your setting and location, you'll also need either natural light, or enough lighting to adequately illuminate the subject (you!)

Video newbies are often surprised to learn that you do not necessarily need a fancy or expensive video camera, and that a webcam or smartphone (i.e. iPhone) is more than enough to get the job done. Most smartphones (and tablets) today have excellent video capabilities, and the convenience factor can't be beat!

People are also surprised to learn that, even though I do video for a living, I mostly use my iPhone or my webcam (embedded in my Mac) as my primary video cameras. The iPhone makes a great video camera, and these days you'll even hear stories of professional, high end commercials and movies being shot using an iPhone. If you're more of a tablet fan, today's iPads also have top notch video recording capability.

When I'm not using my iPhone or iPad to shoot video, I'm likely at my (Mac) computer or laptop using the built-in "iSight" webcam. Again, quality is rarely an issue when using these or other webcams. If you still don't have a desktop or laptop with a webcam built-in, any Logitech or Microsoft webcam is a safe bet.

Most external webcams connect to your computer via USB port, and most can capture audio as well as video. Webcams range in features and price from $30 to $130 US dollars, but even the lower priced models can do the job. At the time of this writing, one of the consistently highest rated webcams is the *Logitech HD Pro Webcam C920*, which retails for about $65 US dollars.

Use What You've Got!

The bottom line when it comes to video cameras is to start where you're at and use what you've got! If you've already got a smartphone with video capabilities, you're ready to roll! I rarely, if ever, encourage my video coaching clients to go out and spend a lot of money on an expensive DLSR (digital single-lens reflex camera), as it's way more "firepower" than the average user needs. DSLR cameras can run into the hundreds or even thousands of dollars, so consider your needs before you invest.

If you're a professional videographer or photographer, you may want a higher end camera, but it's certainly not necessary for most everyday video needs for the typical small business owner. Some of my clients even use older model "handi-cams" or pocket cameras, and I say, "if it works, it works!" Remember our video watch words when it comes to cameras or any video equipment: Keep it simple!

Many effective business videos are created (and distributed) directly from smartphone or tablets, so don't feel any kind of video inferiority complex if you're making videos with your iPhone. A smartphone and a platform for hosting your videos — such as YouTube, Vimeo or Facebook — is really all you need to get going.

Oftentimes, the camera operator is more important than the camera itself. If you're doing a "selfie" video with an iPhone or smartphone, be careful to hold the camera steady. Better yet, use a selfie stick to maintain better control of the camera/phone. If your location allows, use a camera tripod whenever possible. You can easily find an iPhone or smartphone adapter or holder that connects to a traditional camera tripod. This will keep your shot nice and steady.

When it comes to audio, it's often said that it's just as important, if not more so, than video. I find that statement to hold true, as most folks will watch a "bad" picture if the content is compelling, but if the sound is inaudible, the video won't be watched. Make sure the audio on your video is loud and clear!

Audio is also much more difficult, if not impossible, to fix in post production. You may be able to clean up the image in editing, but audio editing is much more challenging. So the lesson is to make sure you've got good audio when you're shooting.

How do you ensure decent sound? First, you test, and make sure your volume is adequate. If you're using a smartphone, you can use the internal microphone when shooting video, but don't get too far away from the phone or the audio will degrade.

If necessary, get an external microphone for your smartphone, such as a lavalier mic. One popular and affordable model is the *Audio-Technica ATR3350 Omnidirectional Condenser Lavalier Microphone* — usually under $30 on Amazon. Another option is the higher end ($70) *Rode smartLav+ Lavalier Microphone* for iPhone and Smartphones. If you prefer to go totally professional (but more expensive), then consider a wireless system from Sennheiser or Movo.

Finally, you'll need a place to "store" or host your videos once they're done. The easy and obvious choice is YouTube, since it's free and offers unlimited hosting of your videos. Tip: If you want to host your video, but you're not ready for the world to see it, make the video private or unlisted on YouTube. Vimeo is another option for hosting your videos, and is often thought to be a higher end choice because there's less "clutter" on the video channel. I often make the analogy that YouTube is the Wal-Mart of video hosting sites, while Vimeo is the Nordstrom!

Additional Tools

We've looked at simple options for your video camera and microphone, but you may be wondering what other tools or equipment you might need to create great video. As is often the case, the answer is "it depends."

First, let's make an important distinction about two types of videos. I often tell my clients that most videos can be divided into two, simple categories, which I call "on the fly" or "keeper."

An "on the fly" video is exactly what it sounds like: A quick, "in-the-moment" video shot on the go or live. An on the fly video is more about the moment and what's happening as you shoot. It can be an event video, an impromptu testimonial video, an on-location video, or a live streaming video such as Facebook Live.

With these videos, content is more important than quality and done is better than perfect. These types of immediate videos may have less of a "shelf life," (and may even expire like Periscope or SnapChat), and the key is to get the video done and posted quickly. Not surprisingly, most "on the fly" videos are created with a mobile device like an iPhone.

"Keeper" videos, on the other hand, are typically going to be more permanent and are usually created with a very specific goal in mind. Think home page video, sales video, product launch videos, etc. Keeper videos need more thought and planner, and should be higher quality than your quick, on the go videos. You can also think of "keeper" videos as branding videos, as they will often reflect your personal brand.

Keeper videos may require more editing and post-production, so you can really control what the final product looks and sounds like. These are the videos that are going to have more "shelf life," and will likely be around for a while — especially if it's something like the "welcome" video on your home page or the "channel trailer" on your YouTube channel.

Once you've made the distinction between "quick" and "keeper" videos, you can better determine your specific equipment needs. On the fly videos, for example, may not require additional lighting or editing. Think of a Facebook Live video, where you may be live streaming from your mobile device and don't have as much control over the lighting or background noise.

Keeper videos that are selling a product or service, and are reflective of your brand, will likely need more production and editing, as you want these videos to look more professional. In this case, you may want additional lighting, control over the background, and possibly music or voice over done during the editing process.

When creating a video that needs to be more professional and polished, consider the use of these additional tools:

- **Lighting** — I recommend "soft box" lighting, which provides adequate light for your videos if you're shooting in a darker location or at night. Most video pros like to use "3-point" lighting (another trick borrowed from television production). 3-point lighting uses a "key" light, or main light source; a "fill" light, often used to eliminate shadows; and a "back" light, to light the background and create some depth between the subject and the background. Many light kits come in sets of three so you can utilize the 3-point lighting scheme.

- **Backgrounds** — With a "keeper" video, you want to have control over your environment and your background. Do you want the background to be part of the message? For example, if you're a medical professional, do you want to shoot in an office or exam room? Or do you prefer a more neutral background. Many videos are shot on a bright white background, made famous by Apple commercials and other top brands. Your video style may call for a black background. Or, if you've got the need for a completely different background, such as an animated or photo background, you may even consider a green screen, where you can replace the green background with any image or graphic in the editing process. Amazon and other retailers sell a background kit that comes with black, white and green for all your needs.

- **Tripod** — Lastly, nothing screams unprofessional like a shaky shot. A shaky or unsteady camera is easily remedied by using a tripod. Most traditional (photo) camera tripods will work fine for video cameras, though you may need any adapter. The folks at caddiebuddy.com produce some excellent iPhone and iPad tripod holders and adapters, for example. Do what you need to do to keep that camera shot steady and stable!

More Cool Tools

There's no shortage of video tools, apps and software, and it can be overwhelming trying to choose the right resources for your video production. We'll be sharing more tools throughout the book but, in the meantime, here are three of our favorites:

Intro Designer: This handy and affordable app is available in the App Store for the iPhone and iPad, and is just $3.99. Intro Designer allows you to create high-end, animated openers, intros, credits and more using their 21 professional templates. You simply choose a pre-made motion graphics template, and replace the generic text with your own. You can customize their templates to create movie trailer style intros, birthday videos, holiday videos, and more! Check out the templates and ideas at http://www.introdesignerapp.com/.

AudioJungle.net: It's usually a struggle to find affordable, royalty-free music for your video productions, but AudioJungle solves that problem. AudioJungle is part of the Envato Market family of resources (http://market.envato.com/), where you can find not only music, but graphics, stock photos, Adobe AfterEffects video templates and more. The music site is my favorite though, with over half a million custom tracks and sound effects to choose from. There's every music style and genre imaginable, and cuts start at just $1, but average about $19.

Adobe Spark: Spark began as Adobe Voice, an iPad app for creating animated videos, but has grown and evolved into a series of mobile apps including Spark Post, for creating social graphics with custom text; Spark Page, for turning words and images into web "stories;" and Spark Video, used for creating animated videos using pre-designed templates. Spark video remains my personal favorite, as it's super simple to record your voice to your iPad, then add photos, graphics, and music from the Spark app. Explore the possibilities at https://spark.adobe.com/

The Rule of Thirds

Even with all the great tools and resources available to you, if you're doing a talking head video, you've still got to "look good" on camera. For a professional presence, you'll want to make sure that your framing, or composition, looks good, and that you're positioned properly in the camera frame. You can use the photographer's "rule of thirds" to make sure that you look good in the shot.

The rule of thirds suggests that you divide your screen into three horizontal and three vertical lines, almost like a tic-tac-toe board. Ideally, the "action" should take place at the intersection of the lines, or the "focal points" within the frame.

And while you may not be running on a beach with a giant green flag as pictured, this image is a good example of using the focal points of the rule of thirds for good visual composition.

For a more typical head and shoulders video shot, you will usually want to make sure the person's eyes are on the top third of the screen, and the person is slightly off center (on the left or right vertical line.

According to Vladimir Gendelman, CEO of CompanyFolders.com, portraits *"work best when the person's eyes overlap with the intersections on a 3x3 grid. Since those intersections are key focal points, this creates a better sense of eye contact and engagement than placing them dead-center."* (see example image)

You should also use the rule of thirds when it comes to graphics or on screen overlays. "Lower thirds" graphics get their name, not surprisingly, because the text occupies the lower third of the screen. You can see this effect at work in most newscasts or talk shows, though networks like ESPN and CNN have taken it to the extreme with lower thirds, scrolling text, logo bugs and other graphics sharing the screen with the on-camera talent.

Video Editing

Editing video often strikes fear into the hearts of most business owners, but you can take solace in the fact that video editing not as difficult as you might imagine. In fact, today's tools make it quicker and easier than ever to edit and embellish your video.

Here are a few things to keep in mind when editing an on-camera video:

- Keep in mind that a little editing goes a long way. You may not need to get too elaborate with your edits.

- Don't add bells and whistles just for the sake of it. You may have editing software that offers 200 different kinds of transitions, but this does not mean you should use all 200 transitions!

- Simple is better: Use simple cuts or dissolves for transitions, minimal graphics, and subtle background music.

- Be sure to trim the front and back (end) of your video is there's unnecessary footage. This is likely where you leaned in to hit the record button.

- Add a lower third graphic when possible. It gives the viewer a visual cue of who or what's on screen.

- Music can set the tone of the video and make it more powerful and emotional. Use music wisely.

- An animated, branded intro and/or "outro" can also make your video look much more professional.

As for video editing platforms, start with the "low hanging fruit" of free and easy video editors, and work your way up to more professional platforms as your videos and your skills evolve. YouTube's free onboard editor is a great place to start because it's easy and intuitive and, chances are, you're uploading your video to YouTube anyway!

If you need a more robust editing option, then check out WeVideo.com, which offers a variety of editing choices online, so it works whether you're on a Mac or a PC. WeVideo even has a free version that includes 1GB of cloud storage and 22 free songs from their music library. WeVideo's paid program starts with a one time payment of $29.99 and gives you more features, including access to 100 songs in their music library.

If you've got an iPad (or a Mac), then Apple's iMovie is a great editing option, with lots of features, flexibility and built-in templates to start with. For more advanced video editing, check out Camtasia or, my favorite and go-to editing platform, Final Cut Pro.

QUICKSTART PRODUCTION GUIDE

For the eager or impatient aspiring videopreneurs among us, we've got some quick tips for getting started with your video production:

- **Choose your camera:** Use your smartphone, a webcam, camcorder — whatever you've got!

- **Find your location:** Choose an appropriate spot to shoot your video, keeping in mind the background and environment.

- **Check your shot:** Be aware of your framing, as well as your lighting (light from the front)

- **Watch your time:** Keep your video as short as possible (under 3 minutes in most cases)

- **Practice your delivery:** You can ad-lib, use a script or a rough outline — Keep it simple!

- **Retake as needed:** It makes sense to rehearse and do retakes, but don't go overboard.

- **Pick your take:** Pick the best take and go with it — it's often the first or last take!

- **Editing optional:** Don't worry too much about the bells and whistles at first. You can grow into that!

On or Off?

Remember our distinction between "Quick" and "Keeper" videos from earlier in this chapter? Well, there's another equally important distinction, or decision, we need to make about video production: Should you create an on-camera video, or an off-camera video?

We'll delve more deeply into this in the next chapter on Video Platforms but, for from a video production standpoint, just know that the on vs. off-camera decision will obviously impact your approach to production. We've focused mostly on traditional on-camera videos in this chapter, because those "talking head" videos usually require the most production.

However, off-camera videos, including animated videos, Power-Point videos, and screencasts, often require a completely different production approach, because most are based on software or specific applications.

Use the chart below to give you a better sense of whether (or when) you need an on camera or off camera production:

ON-CAMERA VIDEOS	OFF-CAMERA VIDEOS
Welcome (Home Page) Video	Webinars/Tutorials/Demos
FAQs or Tips Series	Animated Videos
About Me Video	Explainer Videos
Facebook Live/Livestream Videos	Screencasts (Camtasia)
Interviews/Testimonials	PowerPoint to Video

There's plenty more you should know about various off and on-camera options, and we're going to do a deep dive on many of the tools and resources available to you in Chapter 4, where we discuss "Video Platforms" and finding your "Video Sweet Spot!"

CHAPTER 3 VIDEO KEYS

1. Organize your production into three phases: Pre-Production, Production, and Post-Production

2. Follow a "less is more" approach. Keep it simple!

3. When it comes to cameras and equipment, use what you've got!

4. Determine whether your video is a "quick" or a "keeper" video

5. Use the photographer's "Rule of Thirds" when setting up your video shot

6. Edit as needed — A little editing goes a long way!

Video Platforms: Finding Your Video Sweet Spot and Style

There are so many video styles and platforms available today, it can be overwhelming to try to keep track and sort them all out! Fortunately, we've done that for you...

With the deluge of websites, apps, web plug-ins and tools now available online, the real challenge is not just keeping track of what's out there, but finding the best platform for your specific needs.

I call that your "Video Sweet Spot," and finding it can mean the difference between video success and failure. Your Video Sweet Spot is your "go to" video style or platform. It's the easiest and most effective video platform for you. One that's so seamless for you that it eventually becomes your "default" style video, that you crank out anytime.

The importance finding your own, specific Video Sweet Spot is all about determining a style that works for you — one that you become so comfortable with that video becomes a "no-brainer." One of the big benefits of having a Video Sweet Spot is that, if you're more comfortable with a particular style or platform, you'll be more consistent and make more videos. (More videos = good thing!)

In this chapter, we'll be digging into how to find your Video Sweet Spot and how to use it to your advantage. We'll show you all kinds of video platform options and opportunities, so you can test and experiment, mix and match, and find the right platform for you. That could be on-camera, off-camera, it could be doing video interviews or live streaming, or it could be video animation or screencasts. We'll review various options so you can discover your own go-to style.

On-Camera videos, for example, include all "talking head" videos, such as YouTube tips, video blog posts, sales videos, about me videos, promotional videos and the like.

Live Videos, as the name suggests, include live webcasting or live streaming via Facebook Live, Periscope, YouTube Live, Snapchat and similar apps for creating videos live and on-the-go.

Continuing clockwise around our "video tree," **Hybrid Videos** are a combination of live and screen-sharing videos, such as the videos you can create on Zoom or via Skype, as you toggle between being on camera and sharing your screen.

Animated Videos include video animation created using websites or tools such as Powtoon, GoAnimate, VideoScribe, VideoMakerFX, or other software that we'll review later in this chapter.

Next up are **"Screencasts,"** or screen capture videos typically created with Camtasia, Jing, SnagIt, or voice over slide videos like PowerPoint to video.

And finally, **Photo Montage Videos** are exactly what the name implies: Videos created using a combination of photos (or video clips), music, and text or graphics. These video montages can be produced easily using software such as Animoto or Stupeflix.

What's Your "Video Persona"

We've talked a lot about tools and resources you can use depending on your preference and your Video Sweet Spot, so let's look at one way to determine your sweet spot by identifying your particular "video persona." The following assessment is geared more towards on-camera videos, but knowing your video persona will help you determine what types of videos you should be creating in the first place.

As we've seen, one of the keys to being successful with video marketing is to be sure you're creating the right kind of video for your personality — especially if you plan to create on-camera videos where you're the star.

If you've had mixed results thus far with video, or have yet to tackle video at all, it could be that you're attempting the wrong "type" of video for your personality. In working with hundreds of entrepreneurs over the last several years, I've identified three distinct video "personas" or personality types. What's most fascinating is that there are actually ideal formats and styles of video for each individual video persona.

Why is this important?

By matching your video strategy with your own video persona, you can dramatically increase your chances for success, while saving yourself a lot of time and frustration. Once you've identified your specific video persona, you can gravitate towards the type of videos that are going to be the easiest and the most effective for you to create.

So what are the three video personas, and how do they differ?

The three main video personas are based not only on your level of experience, but also on your personality, your personal style, your comfort level with technology and your ultimate goals. You may instinctively know your video persona, but here's an overview of the three video personas and what types of videos are the best fit for each style:

Video Newbie

Video Newbies have little or no experience with online video, though they understand the importance of establishing a video presence. Most Video Newbies would rather get a root canal than be in front of the camera, though in most cases, a little practice is all they need. Video Newbies also tend to be "technophobes," since they don't yet realize that there are many low-tech options for creating video.

The best type of videos for most Video Newbies include a brief "welcome" video for your home page, or "off-camera" videos such as photo montages, screencasts, or narrated PowerPoint videos. Obviously, Video Newbies need the most guidance and support, and can benefit most from online courses or personal coaching.

Video Explorer

Video Explorers are a bit more adventurous, and like to "do it themselves" — or at least know how to do it themselves. Video Explorers usually have some experience with video, though their initial forays into video may have been frustrating. Explorers are less intimidated by cameras and equipment, and most consider themselves relatively tech-savvy. Video Explorers are independent and determined to figure it out. Sometimes the "DIY" attitude of the Video Explorer can actually work against them, since even a little help can give them a big boost.

Best videos for Video Explorers include an on-camera video tips series, off-camera screencast demos or instructional videos, and promotional videos to promote products, services, webinars or events. Video Explorers are usually more comfortable experimenting with new tools and resources that satisfy their independent nature. However, Explorers can also benefit from coaching or support to sometimes help them "get out of their own way."

Videopreneur

Videopreneurs are the more experienced, marketing-savvy professionals. They've been in the game for a while and are always hungry for the latest, greatest tools and short-cuts. They realize that video is a means to an end, and that the content of their videos is far more important than the technology. Videopreneurs have had some success with video, but realize that there's much more they could — and should — be doing. Videopreneurs are on the vanguard and are on their way to becoming consistent content producers.

Best videos for Videopreneurs include just about any video content, though on-camera videos are typically much more effective (and satisfying) for this personality type. For Videopreneurs, the style of video is not nearly as important as the video marketing strategy. Videopreneurs can enjoy continued and growing success by developing an overall video strategy that's tied to their long term goals. Videopreneurs benefit from a consistent strategy for content-rich videos to enhance their credibility and engage their followers.

The Match Game

As you can imagine, a Video Newbie who is somewhat camera shy is going to struggle if they decide to create a weekly videoblog series. While that's not the ideal format for a Newbie, off-camera screen-cast tutorials or photo/video montages may be perfect for the video beginner.

And a Newbie isn't going to be a Newbie for long. Once the less-experienced producer gets a few videos under his or her belt, they may quickly jump to the "Explorer" persona. Video Explorers are going to dabble and try on several video formats until they find one that fits. But don't be fooled into thinking you're a Newbie just because you're an introvert. There are many savvy Videopreneurs who are also quite shy – They've just found a process and strategy that works for them. Again, it's all a matter of finding that video "sweet spot" which will give you the best results based on your own video persona.

Knowing your style and understanding the ideal video plan for your persona can mean the difference between video frustration and video success. Whatever your results may be, the important thing is to find out what kind of videos work best for you so you can benefit from video marketing and actively participate in the online video revolution.

On-Camera Videos

At the end of Chapter 3, we talked about the difference between on-camera and off-camera videos. Now it's time to take a closer look at both options so we can begin to determine your Video Sweet Spot. We'll start with the most obvious and traditional video style: On-Camera.

Appearing on camera in your videos is arguably the most powerful and compelling online video format, because so real and "present." With on-camera videos, you can use the force of your personality, even if your more of an introvert, or the "strong, silent type." There's no better way to make an authentic, personal connection with your audience than with on-camera videos.

Being on camera is also the best vehicle for building the all-important "know, like and trust" factor with your viewers, because your sharing yourself and engaging your viewer. Talking directly to your viewers on camera is "relationship" marketing, and is, in most cases, the next best thing to in-person, face to face communications.

On-camera videos, often referred to as "talking head" videos, are also best for establishing your online visibility, since it's you who's appearing on camera and becoming more familiar and recognized to your audience. This type of "up close and personal" video is also great for establishing your credibility and expert status. If you want to be seen as the authority in your niche, you've got to be front and center on camera.

While there may be hundreds of ways to create videos, there's simply no substitute for showing up on camera. There's a reason why major brands spend millions to make professional athletes and celebrities their on-camera spokespeople: Being on camera makes an immediate, dynamic and visceral connection. And that's good news because, for some situations, you simply must be on-camera.

When to Use...

Those "must be on camera" videos include your website's main home page or "welcome" video, particularly if you are your business, or you're the face of your business. Your welcome video on your website is your "first impression" video, so it's best that you appear on camera to make that initial, personal connection.

On camera videos also include your "about me" video, where you've got the opportunity to share your story and background with your viewer. The "about" video is often a missed opportunity for entrepreneurs, since most small business owners usually settle for a standard text bio. Why not bring your website's "about me" page to life with a more compelling *video* version of that bio?

In fact, you can make all your web pages or landing pages more personal and inviting by adding an on-camera video. For example, in addition to creating a persuasive sales video where you appear on camera, you can also include an on-camera video on your "Thank

You" page after your customer opts-in to your mailing list or buys your product. Thank you page videos are the perfect opportunity to express your appreciation to your customer and ensure that the customer has made a wise decision.

And if you're doing a live event or an online webinar, a more personal, on-camera video on your web pages can increase attendance and conversions, because you're making your event more authentic and inviting. Anytime you include an on-camera video on one of your web pages, whether it's an "about" page, a "thank you" page, or even a "contact us" page, you're validating the viewer's online experience, making it more authentic, and giving your viewer the promise that "you've got their back!"

Other instances where you'll want to appear on camera include your "expert tips" video series, where you're sharing your knowledge and expertise on YouTube or on your own website or blog. These tips videos not only add value for your target market, but they also position you as the expert and authority in your field.

For the most part, any kind of live video, online panel discussion or video interview is going to be an on-camera video, such as when you're doing a Facebook Live video or livestream video. This includes webcasting and videoconferencing, like the multi-screen/multi-person videos you can create using a video service such as zoom.us.

You can also be on camera to create Video Emails, which are becoming more mainstream and more popular with services such as MailVu.com. V-Mail is an ideal way to make a more personal and intimate connection with a colleague or client. Your video email will easily stand out among the hundreds of other regular emails your customers receive.

Keep in mind that you can plug in on-camera videos just about anywhere in your marketing, whether it's for video blog posts, video webinars, product demos or tutorial videos, as well as on-camera videos for a product launch series. Think about where you can bolster your business by adding personal, on-camera videos.

What's Your Video Sweet Spot?

You may know you're a natural on camera, or you may have to stretch past your comfort zone to find the right "video voice" for you, but once you do find your video sweet spot, the process of creating videos becomes much easier!

- Do you prefer video over writing? Do video blog posts.

- Do you like teaching? Create a video tips series.

- If you like live interaction, try a video interview.

- Are you more of a storyteller? Then maybe an animated video is more your style.

- Or are you determined to build a following or fan base? You'll need a compelling opt-in video!

Don't be afraid to try different video styles to find your Video Sweet Spot...

Live Video

The use of live video has absolutely exploded, thanks in large part to Facebook Live, which has taken live streaming video to the masses.

Some of the Facebook Live highlights worth noting are that *videos have 135% greater organic reach* on Facebook compared to photo posts, and that *Facebook has an average of 8 Billion daily video views.*

Clearly, Facebook Live has changed the game when it comes to video. Today, anyone with a smartphone or computer can be broadcasting live video on Facebook in a matter of two clicks on their screen. And that's exactly what millions of people are doing every day!

Of course, there are other live video platforms, most notably Periscope, Instagram, Snapchat, and even Twitter, but Facebook is clearly king when it comes to live video, if for no other reason that pretty much everyone already uses the social network. And it didn't take long for YouTube and Twitter to up their live video game, but Facebook seems to be the platform of choice for the majority of folks using live video.

The popularity of Facebook Live could be attributed to it's incredible ease of use. Especially on mobile devices, Facebook has made shooting a live video as easy as snapping a picture. And, Facebook continues to evolve and update their Live video capabilities by adding Snapchat like features and filters, along with other bells and whistles to make Facebook Live videos more fun and engaging.

Facebook Live is also a great way to wade into the video waters, even if you're a video newbie — both because of it's ease of use and it's informal, "in-the-moment" nature. I'll stop short of saying that Facebook Live has lowered the bar on video, but now that anyone can create a video anytime... anyone can create a video anytime! (And that's not always a good thing!) Still, the "video intimidation" factor seems to be lower.

Facebook Live could be described as a "come as you are" video, with little need for pre-production, and rarely any need for post-production or editing. It's about as "point and shoot" easy as it can be! That's why I often recommend Facebook Live as a first stop for those just beginning to attempt on-camera videos. With Facebook Live's privacy settings, you've also got the option to share your video to specific groups, or even to "only me" if you prefer to do a practice run.

Finally, there's no better reason to do Facebook Live videos than the fact that Facebook gives them so much prominence. Facebook loves video, and there's nothing more "newsfeed-worthy" than Facebook Live videos. Facebook founder Mark Zuckerberg himself calls video a "mega-trend," and states that he "wouldn't be surprised if you fast-forward five years and most of the content that people are sharing on a day-to-day basis is video."

Which Type of Posts Get the Most Engagement for Brands

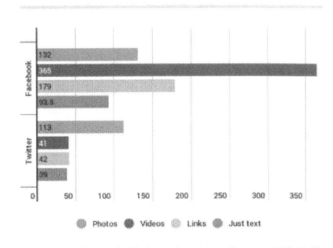

● Photos ● Videos ● Links ● Just text

≋ buffer

Facebook has doubled-down on video, and you should, too! Posting videos and going live from Facebook will give you more reach, more visibility and more engagement. For further proof, look at these statistics provided by Buffer on which type of posts get the most engagement. As you can see, video on Facebook leaves all other content in the dust!

Top 10 Tips for Maximizing Live Video

1. Seize the moment — Live video is the perfect vehicle for "in the moment," on-the-fly videos, so be sure to use it whenever the moment strikes you. Live video captures those spontaneous, sharable moments, and all you need is your mobile device!

2. Engage! — Live video is ideal for engaging your audience, so be sure to acknowledge your viewers, give shout-outs to those who join, make them part of the broadcast and make your livestream interactive. Live video is a two-way street!

3. Go live on Twitter — Facebook Live is the king of live video, but let's not forget that we can also go live right from Twitter, thanks to Periscope (which Twitter owns). You don't even need the Periscope app to use the live video feature on Twitter, which broadcasts your video right in the stream!

4. Enhance your live broadcasts with third party apps — You can put your live webcasts on steroids with third-party software and resources like OBS (Open Broadcaster Software) at obsproject.com, or BeLive.tv. OBS allows you to add multiple cameras and graphics to your Facebook Live broadcasts, while BeLive adds the option of doing two-person broadcasts, along with a Q&A function that overlays viewer comments on the screen.

5. Be consistent — One and done won't really get it done when it comes to building visibility and engagement with live video. Try to go live often, or make a commitment to do a regular "appointment view-ing" webcast once a week (or once a day if you're more ambitious!)

6. Try different livestream formats — Such as video interviews, Q&A live sessions, or "behind the scenes" webcasts. Experiment with different content and styles until you find your live sweet spot.

7. Add Instagram to your live mix — Instagram may be best known for posting photos, but you can also post 3 to 60-second videos on the social platform, as well! And with Instagram's 600 million monthly users, it's another great way to get video visibility!

8. Start with a plan — You don't need a script to go live, but you should have a pretty good idea of what you're going to say, do or show. Facebook Live and other live video platforms may be instantaneous and in-the-moment, but that doesn't mean you should totally wing it

9. Promote your live broadcasts — Live any live event, your livestream should be promoted in advance if you want to build buzz and awareness for your broadcast. While this might not be practical for impromptu videos, you can certainly let your audience know if you've got a live video pre-scheduled.

10. Follow up after the fact — Once your live broadcast is over, your work is not necessarily done. Spread and share your video recording as appropriate: Cross post to your other social networks and leverage your video for additional views and greater visibility.

Follow these guidelines along with you own intuition and you'll be able to make the most of all the opportunities live videos offer!

FACEBOOK LIVE CHECKLIST

PRE-BROADCAST

- Check your Internet connection/Wifi
- Check your battery charge on your phone
- Turn on airplane mode or do not disturb
- Be sure to pre-promote your broadcast
- Let your followers know when you're going live!
- Check your lighting and audio
- Use a tripod to keep your phone steady and stable
- Write a compelling headline/description to attract viewers

BROADCAST

- "Hook" your viewers in the first few seconds
- Why should they watch?
- Have a plan and purpose from the start
- Consider going live for 5 – 20 minutes
- Acknowledge your viewers by name with "shout-outs"
- Interact and answer viewer questions
- Ask your viewers to subscribe to future broadcasts

- Include a Call to Action before signing off
- Tell your viewers what you want them to do next!

POST BROADCAST

- Save your broadcast to your camera roll
- Save an HD/higher quality version if possible
- Share the replay on your other Facebook pages and groups (Use a service like "Live Leap")
- Download the broadcast so you can repurpose and share on other platforms
- Continue to respond to questions and comments on the replay
- Edit your video (Choose thumbnail, add captions, etc)
- Consider uploading to YouTube or Vimeo
- Consider creating a :30 version for Twitter
- Consider creating a :60 version for Instagram

When to Use...

Live video can be used almost anytime, from anywhere. And if you're going live from your mobile device, it's even easier and more convenient to do those spur-of-the-moment live videos. More specific uses for live, on-the-fly videos include:

On location — Simply pull out your iPhone or mobile device and hit record — wherever, whenever you are at a cool location or special spot you want to share!

Live interviews — Perhaps you're at a conference or an industry event and you run into someone who's perfect to interview right then and there. Or, you can just as easily do a live interview if your guest is at another location. Live video is ideal for interviews or panel discussions.

Q&A with viewers — Third party apps like BeLive.tv for Facebook Live make it super simple to conduct live Q&A broadcasts, where your audience can interact and ask their questions live on the webcast.

Special events — Events and occasions are perfect opportunities to go live. You can capture the action with your mobile device and "share" the event live with your viewers.

Behind the scenes — People love being taken "behind the scenes" and seeing what's happening "off screen." Give your viewers a glimpse backstage or share some rarely seen footage to make them feel like VIPs.

Share the moment — Any occasion — business, personal, unique or fun — can be turned into a live video that you share with your viewers. Next time you experience something, especially when it's something visual, capture the moment and share it with your followers.

Announcements — Have you got a big announcement you can share live? Maybe a new product coming out, or a special milestone your business is celebrating? Share the excitement and the news with a live video!

Hybrid Videos

At the intersection of live videos and screen recordings is a video style I call "hybrid" videos. Hybrid videos are simply a combination of live, on-camera videos and off-camera screencasts or screen sharing.

Hybrid videos offer the best of both worlds, because you get the closeness and "connection" of being on camera, along with the ability to switch over to sharing your computer screen for demos, slide shows, or whatever else you want to display to your audience.

This style of toggling back and forth between appearing on camera and showing your screen can be very effective and engaging, and it's a great way to keep the interest and attention of your viewer. It's also a great way to conduct video webinars, since you can appear on camera of your webinar introduction; switch over to your slides on screen; then pop back on camera for a more personal close to your online event.

Hybrid videos are my personal favorite, and often my go-to style for sharing tips, tutorials or a lot of information. Sharing my Power-Point slides on screen is an effective way to get a lot of content out there, and the ability to switch back to my "talking head" shot on camera keeps the audience more connected to the event.

You can create those combo videos using various types of software, most notably zoom.us and similar video conferencing solutions. Most will allow you to stay on screen via "picture in picture," but I prefer to either be full screen on camera or full screen on my slides. It's really a matter of personal preference.

You can also produce hybrid videos using Skype, Go To Webinar, WebinarJam, and other third party resources. Each has its own features and benefits, but I usually recommend Zoom to my clients because of it's ease of use and it's generous free version — where you can host up to 50 participants on a 40 minute video conference. Once your video goes over 40 minutes, you'll have to upgrade to one of Zoom's paid plans, which start at just $14.99 per month.

While Zoom gets my personal recommendation, it is not the only video conferencing solution.

Video Hacks

Video marketing can be incredibly effective for entrepreneurs and small business owners who need to compete with bigger, better funded competitors. Promoting your business with video can level the playing field and give you a huge advantage because video builds the "know, like and trust" factor and accelerates the sales process.

However, many entrepreneurs feel that video marketing is beyond their reach because it can be so time consuming and complicated. Many people are missing out on the online video revolution because they fear the time commitment of doing video.

Fortunately, video does not have to take a ton of time or effort. There are all kinds of shortcuts and hacks for making video simple.

Here are my 6 favorite video productivity tips:

1. That Jing Thing — Go download Jing at https://www.techsmith. com/jing.html. (Free) This simple sibling of Camtasia is more than a screen capture tool. You can also instantly record your screen for up to 5 minutes. It's perfect for quick screencast videos or mini-slide shows. Just fire it up and start talking over your computer screen. Best of all: The 5 minute limit keeps you focused and succinct... a must for videos!

2. Zoom in on video — If you prefer to be on camera, or if you want the flexibility of being able to toggle between on camera and screen sharing, then zoom.us is the perfect solution. Zoom offers video conferencing and online meetings, but more important, video recording. (Free for up to 40 minutes; Pro Plans start at $14.99/month). You can host up to 50 participants on the free plan, but the real "hack" here is to use it as a video recording tool. Record yourself or your screen (even with no participants), and you've got a fast and easy video!

3. Go Live — Facebook Live, Periscope and now, Instagram all give you the ability to broadcast live with just your smartphone. With just a couple of taps on your phone, this may be the quickest and easiest way to create a video. And because platforms like Facebook Live are designed to be recorded "in the moment" and on the fly, there's no need nor expectation for fancy editing or post production. Just hit record and go!

4. Montage Mania — Having a bad hair day or don't want to appear on camera? Then simply pull together a few photos and create a quick photo/video montage. Low and no cost tools like stupeflix.com animoto.com and Adobe Spark for the iPad (https://spark.adobe.com/) make it super simple to upload images or graphics and add words and music to create a great video. These services even provide stock photos, themes and free music to go along with your montage.

5. Vmail is the new Email — Video email is far more engaging and effective than traditional email, because you get to connect directly with your viewer in a much more personal way. Email is perfect for direct outreach or follow up after a meeting or event, and it's as simple as talking into your webcam or smartphone. MailVu.com and eyejot.

com both offer free versions, while services like bombbomb.com start at $39.99 per month if you need lots of bells and whistles.

6. PowerPoint to Video — Whether you're using PowerPoint on a PC, or Screenflow on a Mac, you can narrate and record your slide presentation and save it as a video. This is a great way to repurpose your existing assets if you have any PowerPoint presentations, and it's also the ideal way to conduct webinars.

Cranking out great video doesn't have to be a chore. Use any of these time-saving video hacks and watch your video productivity soar!

Off-Camera Videos

Now that we've teased you with a short preview of some off-camera options mentioned in our "video hacks" section, it's time to take a closer look at videos you can create without having to appear on camera.

Off camera videos give you a tremendous amount of flexibility and a wide range of options. This type of video is ideal for teaching and demonstrating, such as video tutorials or instructional videos. They are also a great way to deliver a webinar or present a lot of information. (You can use slides and graphics to visually illustrate your points.) You've also got the opportunity to create unique and memorable videos using off-camera methods, whether it's animation, the popular "sketch" style videos, explainer videos or photo/video montages.

Some of the distinct advantages of off camera videos include the simple fact that you don't need to appear on camera! That means no need for hair and make-up, no need for special lighting, and no need to worry about your background or setting. In many cases, off camera videos are quicker, easier and less hassle than on camera efforts.

Off camera videos also provide a nice change of pace from your typical "talking head" videos, and they can also be ideal for repurposing existing content. A written blog post or article, for example, can be given new life as a PowerPoint video with voice over. In fact, any kind of product demo or teaching video can make a compelling off camera video.

When to Use...

Images and music alone can create engaging storytelling videos; animation can be perfect to explain an idea or concept; and screen sharing videos can provide step-by-step walk throughs of your product or service. Here are some specific ways you can utilize off camera methods:

- *Webinar or video conference*- Best way to delivery lots of information

- *Demo video* — Teaching or training using slides (PowerPoint)

- *Animation* — Creative ways to present ideas and concepts

- *Photo montage* — Can be used to tell a story with photos

- *Screencasts* — Capture or highlight your computer screen

- *Promotional* — "Sizzle" reel, speaker video, promo reel

- *Portfolio* — Show off your work with screen shots, graphics or images

Other popular uses for off camera videos include the widely used "explainer" videos, which are typically videos created with motion graphics or animation. Animated text videos are referred to as "kinetic type" videos, which is another popular style.

"Sketch" or whiteboard videos are also seen often, where animated words or images are drawn on the screen. More traditional animation or cartoon-style videos continue to be popular, as are the "montage" videos created using words, images and music.

Video Tools

By now, you're head may be spinning with ideas for creating off camera videos. But how do you go about actually creating these DIY masterpieces? That's where our video tools and resources come in, and we've got a lot to choose from! Here are my tried, true and tested sources for creating off camera videos. In the spirit of finding your video sweet spot, I'll organize the tools by video style:

Animation

Let's begin with traditional, cartoon-style animation. It wasn't so long ago that it would take a team of animators hours and hours to produce one minute of animation. "Back in the day," when I worked for children's television producer Saban Entertainment and the Fox Kids Network, we'd outsource animation overseas and have to wait weeks to complete a finished cartoon.

With the tools we have now, you can look like a professional animator in a matter of minutes, with little or no learning curve. You're only limited by your imagination!

Start with **Powtoon** (https://www.powtoon.com/) created "so everyone can animate," as their tagline reads. Even with their robust free version, you can choose from 16 styles, access 46 different soundtracks, and create an animation up to 5 minutes in length. Powtoon's basic paid plan ($19/mo) removes the Powtoon watermark and outro, and gives you 24 styles to choose from, 88 music cuts, and up to 15 minutes in length.

While Powtoon is my go-to choice for cartoon-style animation, another viable option is **GoAnimate** (https://goanimate.com/). While they do offer a 14-day free trial, GoAnimate is pricier, with plans starting at $39/month or $299/year.

GoAnimate is arguably more business-focused, offering animated infographics templates, along with whiteboard animation, Common Craft (paper cutout) style videos, and even the ability to import your PowerPoint into the software so you can jazz it up. One other unique feature of GoAnimate is their Automatic Lip-Sync function, where you can assign a voice over to your cartoon character and have it automatically lip-sync.

Screencasts

Screencasts or screen capture videos are a popular and relatively simple way to produce off-camera videos. They're ideal for teaching or demonstration videos, since you can essentially record anything and everything that you're showing on your computer screen. In addition, most screen capture software also allows you to edit and embellish your screen recordings.

The best known screen capture software is also the industry standard: **Camtasia**. In fact, many people use Camtasia not only as a screen capture tool, but also as their primary video editor.

Camtasia has versions for both Mac and PC (though the PC version is more robust), and they also offer a free 30-day trial. The software is priced at $199 USD.

In addition to Camtasia's screen recording feature, the software's editing capabilities have come a long way and now offer drag and drop editing, animated backgrounds, music tracks, and even motion graphics. You can get a full preview of Camtasia's features and sign up for the free trial at https://www.techsmith.com/camtasia.html.

If you're just looking for screen recording without all the bells and whistles, Techsmith (the maker of Camtasia) also offers a less expensive screen capture software called **Snagit** (https://www.techsmith.com/screen-capture.html) This stripped-down version offers a 15-day free trial and retails for $49.95.

An even more streamlined solution from Techsmith is **Jing**, (https://www.techsmith.com/jing.html) a free download that allows both static screen captures, as well as video screen recordings up to 5 minutes in length.

Finally, for Mac users, there's a viable alternative to the somewhat limited Camtasia for the Mac in **Screenflow**, (https://www.telestream.net/screenflow/overview.htm) a full-featured screen recording and editing software specifically for the Mac. Screenflow also offers a free trial, or you can buy the software for $99 USD.

Slide Shows (PowerPoint to Video)

While Camtasia and Screenflow can be used to record and narrate your **PowerPoint** (or Keynote for Mac) presentations, creating video slides shows can also be achieved by simply using PowerPoint or Keynote on their own.

Both Microsoft PowerPoint and Apple's Keynote allow you not only to save your slide presentation in a video format, but they also give you the option to record live narration or voice over with your slides. I use this feature on Keynote for the Mac quite often, as it's a simple, streamlined way to get a clean recording for a video tutorial or webinar.

Photo Montage

One of the easiest ways to create an off camera video is by putting together a photo/video montage. Simple photos, words and music can often combine to make a powerful and emotional video. My two, go-to resources for producing montage videos are Animoto and Stupeflix.

Animoto (https://animoto.com/) has been around for a long time, and continues to lead the way when it comes to producing video graphics and slide shows. They offer dozens of video styles, or templates, to choose from, along with thousands of music cuts to add your soundtrack.

With Animoto, you can create a brief, 30-second video for free, or sign up for one of their paid plans that start at $8 per month if you pay annually. They also offer a free, 14-day trial. Animoto's numerous video styles offer a lot of flexibility to plug in your photos or video clips, and their "Professional" plan ($22/mo) removes the Animoto branding and gives you another 20 templates to choose from.

Stupeflix (https://studio.stupeflix.com/en/) is another viable option for creating professional montage-style videos. In some ways, Stupeflix is a better alternative than Animoto, because Stupeflix allows you to use their 16 themes or styles and create a video of up to 20 minutes for free! Stupeflix also offers music clips, video clips, and the ability to add titles or captions. In addition, Stupeflix makes it easy to upload your video to YouTube or Facebook, or to share or embed your video.

Sketch/Whiteboard

Another very popular off camera style is the "sketch" or whiteboard video. This particular variety was made popular with the increasing availability and affordability of software like VideoScribe, Commoncraft, Explaindio and VideoMakerFX.

VideoScribe (http://www.videoscribe.co/) was first on the scene and set the standard for whiteboard-style animations. Using Video-Scribe, you can add images, text and music in a variety of "hand drawn" styles for a very profession look in minutes. Of course, you can also add voice over to produce an explainer video. It's very user friendly and is reasonably affordable at $12 USD per month (paid annually). When your "scribe" is complete, you can publish it to YouTube, Facebook or PowerPoint. When you buy VideoScribe, you also receive their "Tawe" product, which turns photos into videos or unique presentations – also ideal for quickly animating sketch notes or diagrams.

Commoncraft (https://www.commoncraft.com/) is another popular video style, and has created a category all its own. The unique, cut-out style of videos they create are perfect for "explainer" videos and are especially popular with educators. Commoncraft offers 88 "ready-made" explainer videos, as well as a library of almost 2,500 cut outs you can use to create presentation visuals from scratch. Plans start at $49 USD per year, and they also offer discounted plans for non-profits and schools.

Explaindio (http://explaindio.com/fe/) began as an animated whiteboard creation tool, but has since evolved into creating 2D and 3D animation and motion video. Fees are $59 USD per year, or $69 for a "commercial license that allows you to create and sell your videos. Explaindio gives you 200 "pre-done" animated scenes and 800 doodle sketch images.

Finally, **VideoMakerFX** (http://www.loubortone.com/video-maker — affiliate link) is one of my favorite tools for creating animated videos, character videos and whiteboard videos. VideoMakerFX is easier to use than Expaindio, and more affordable for just a one-time fee of $67 USD. VideoMakerFX works on Mac or PC, the video themes and templates are easily customizable, and they even offer 20 music tracks to add sound to your animations. Of all the many animation tools out there, VideoMakerFX is the one I recommend most often.

Other Tools

There are a few off camera tools that don't really fit into any video category, other than that they're really fun, easy and affordable (or free!) Here's an overview of my three faves:

Adobe Spark

Adobe Spark (https://spark.adobe.com/), formerly Adobe Voice, is an amazing — and free — video storytelling resource for iOS (iPad and iPhone.) Spark's flexibility, ease of use and pre-designed templates make it a no-brainer as a video creation tool.

While Adobe Voice was limited to creating animation on the iPad, Adobe Spark has evolved into an even more useful resource, with three distinct, design uses: **Spark Post** allows you to create great-looking social graphics, using photos, text, and design filters that are all fully customizable.

Spark Page can be used to create responsive, magazine-style web pages, or what Adobe calls "web stories" — which is essentially a one-page website.

Finally, **Spark Video**, the original app, is a simple and lightening fast way to create animations, using your voice, text, graphics or icons (provided inside the app), and music. There's virtually no learning curve, as Spark Video is intuitive and includes several, pre-made styles to get you started. You simply record your voice narration, match up your voice with text and/or graphics from their library, and select some background music. There are 32 styles or themes to choose from. Of course, you can share your finished creation to Twitter or Facebook, send it via email or text message, or embed it on your website.

Intro Designer

Another "ninja" video creation tool, specifically for the iPhone, is **IntroDesigner** (http://www.introdesignerapp.com/#). This handy and affordable ($3.99) app gives you access to 54 professional animation templates that you can customize with your own text or titles. In three quick steps: choose-customize-export, you can create flashy intros, openers, credits and more. There are pre-made templates for birthday and special occasion videos, as well as some more generic title sequences you can customize to create your show open or intro animation. All in all, it's a handy app for four bucks!

Prezi

One other tool that defies a category, though it could fall into the "PowerPoint" realm, is **Prezi.**

Prezi is a unique presentation tool that you can use to take your typical PowerPoint deck to a whole new level with dynamic movement and engaging animations. Prezi presentations feature a map-like, schematic overview that lets users move or pan between topics, zoom in on text and details, and pull back to reveal context.

Prezi's more free-flowing, visual storytelling style is a nice alternative to traditional slide-based formats like PowerPoint and Keynote. Press provides a large library of templates and designs to get you started, and they offer several pricing plans depending on your needs. Plans range from $4.92 to $20.00 per month (paid annually), and all plans include a 14-day free trial.

Best Practices

- Your video marketing objective should determine your platform.

- There's no "one" single best platform. You get to decide!

- Try different styles until you find your "go to" platform.

- Your favorite "default" platform is your Video Sweet Spot!

- Try to use a combination of on-camera and off-camera videos.

- Most (if not all) of your "must have" videos will be on camera.

CHAPTER 4 VIDEO KEYS:

1. Your Video "Sweet Spot" is the video style or platform that you're most comfortable with, and the one that's most appropriate for promoting and marketing your business.

2. You may find that your "Sweet Spot" is a type of on-camera video, whether live or recorded; or you may discover that you prefer one of the many "off-camera" methods.

3. Live video has become extremely popular, thanks in large part to the availability and simplicity of Facebook Live. Other social platforms, such as Instagram and Twitter, now offer live video options.

4. For the best of both worlds, you might consider doing a "hybrid" video, which is a combination of live, on-camera and off-camera screencasts or screen-sharing. Software such as zoom.us can easily give you this flexibility.

5. There are also dozens of off-camera video styles, from cartoon animation and "whiteboard" drawing videos to screencasts and photo/video montages. It's best to explore various software options to find which work best for you.

Video Promotion:
Sharing and Distributing Your Videos
for Maximum Reach

Get It Off the Hard Drive!

Now we get to the fun part: Sharing your video with the world!

You've set your video goals, honed your message, tackled your equipment needs, and found your video sweet spot... So you've got your video; now it's time to get it off your hard drive and out into the world!

Your finished video is not really finished until you share it — as in post, upload, distribute and promote. Even the best videos are useless if they never make it off your hard drive. So your job now is to get your video in front of as many eyeballs as possible! And that means taking your video file (typically an MP4 or .mov file), and uploading it to YouTube, Facebook, Vimeo, and/or putting your video on your own website or blog.

Actually, there are dozens of places to post your video once it's done, so it's really a matter of determining the best destination for your video. That destination could be a video channel like YouTube or Vimeo; it could be a social media platform like Facebook or LinkedIn; or it could be putting the video on your blog or in an email. (Better yet, all of the above!)

The best place to start your video sharing is to go where your target market is! Is your audience on Facebook or LinkedIn? Are they YouTube users? Are they more likely to be found on Instagram or Pinterest? Start where you can get the most impact and go from there.

I often advise my clients to start by uploading their videos to YouTube. Since it's the world's second largest search engine and the "big kahuna" of video sites, it's the obvious choice as a starting point. In addition, it's free video hosting, so it's a great place to store your videos and use as a hub for all your videos.

YouTube (along with most other social sites) makes it very easy to share and distribute your video right from the YouTube platform. Once your video is uploaded to YouTube, you can share with one click to LinkedIn, Google + , Pinterest, etc. (You can also share to Facebook, but it's best to upload natively, i.e. separately, to Facebook — More about that later!)

I See You Everywhere!

Those four short words are music to an entrepreneur's ear: "I see you everywhere!" When you hear that, you know you're on the right track! And the best way to create the "I see you everywhere" effect is to get your videos posted and shared. Your videos can be out there working for you, getting you visibility and exposure, 24/7, all over the world!

To help you achieve the coveted "see you everywhere" effect, we're going to focus this chapter on video visibility strategies, video sharing and distribution, leveraging your videos for maximum impact, and the benefits of "social video."

Video is the perfect vehicle to create that "get seen/get known" factor, because video establishes an immediate, personal and powerful connection to your clients and prospects. Nothing works more quickly or more effectively than video for dramatically increasing your crucial "know, like and trust" factor. And once you've built that trust with video, you can accelerate the sales process and make more money, more quickly!

The importance of creating that bond and connection with your audience cannot be understated. Ultimately, video becomes your tool for building relationships. While it could take weeks, months or years to build trust and forge that bond with your prospects, video marketing has the ability to create relationships practically overnight. That's thanks to video's ability to break through the clutter and make you more memorable. When used properly, video becomes your best sales and marketing strategy.

As you create your videos — particularly your on-camera videos — you become more familiar to your prospects and followers. The more they see you on video, the more they feel like they "know" you. The intimate nature of video only strengthens that connection. That's why it's so important to use video as often as possible to get yourself "out there" and become a trusted advisor to your prospects.

Video Visibility

One of the strongest arguments for using video more consistently is it's ability to increase your online visibility exponentially. Your video gives you a global presence, 24/7 — working for you even while you sleep! Creating and distributing videos is akin to cloning yourself and creating an "army of appearances" across the Internet.

Video generates tremendous awareness and exposure for you and your products and services. So it stands to reason that more video means more awareness! When used strategically, video will dramatically increase your online presence.

Of course, the key to video visibility is video *distribution*. Your awareness will only increase as you get your video "out there" into the world. It's vital to share and distribute your video as widely as possible.

Obviously, you'll upload your video to YouTube and put it on your own website or blog, but that's just the first step. Share your video across all your social platforms. Post your video on Facebook, Pinterest, LinkedIn and your other social networks. Thanks to YouTube's sharing feature, spreading your video to other platforms is often as easy as one click!

You really have to make a conscious effort (with every video) to think beyond YouTube. Where else can you share or "recycle" your video for additional visibility? Consider Instagram, Twitter, Tumblr, etc. Leave no stone unturned! Video plus social media is a powerful combination.

My own video distribution workflow is as follows:

I start by uploading my video to YouTube, using that as my "hub." From there, it's just one click to share the video from YouTube to Twitter, Pinterest, LinkedIn and Google +. I upload the video "natively," or directly to Facebook, because Facebook prefers direct uploads and will give your video more prominence. Finally, I look at other social platforms if appropriate, such as Instagram or Snapchat.

Keep in mind Facebook's relatively recent (and significant) emphasis on video. In fact, Facebook founder Mark Zuckerberg calls video a "megatrend," and the company has put enormous resources into making the social network a video-driven platform. Zuckerberg has been quoted as saying that he "wouldn't be surprised if you fast-forward five years and most of the content that people are sharing on a day-to-day basis is video."

Need more proof that Facebook is "all in" when it comes to video — especially live video? Check out these statistics from *MediaKix:*

- Video on social media generates 1200% more shares than text and images combined.

- Users comment on Facebook Live videos at 10X the rate of regular videos.

- Facebook Live videos are watched 3X longer than those that aren't live anymore.

- 8 Billion daily views for Facebook Video = 100% growth in six months.

- Facebook videos have increased 360% across everyone's news feed.

- Facebook video posts have increased by 94% annually in the U.S.

Zuckerberg recently doubled-down on his bet on video, saying: *"We see a world that is video first, with video at the heart of all of our apps and services"*

Facebook is already the second largest site for watching videos, giving YouTube a real run for its money. Other social platforms are taking a cue from Facebook, and putting much more emphasis on video content. Twitter Live and Instagram Live both give users new opportunities to create live streaming videos right from within their respective platforms, and live streaming video is becoming more and more mainstream. Resources like BeLive.tv and smiletime.com make it even easier to create your own "show" on the web.

Social Video

I've been using the phrase "social video" for years as a way to describe the integration of video and social media. Social video has become more popular as leveraging videos across several social platforms has become more common. The idea behind social video is simply to make your videos as "sharable" as possible and maximize your video distribution.

In the last few years, "social video" has become a buzzword, and brands have embraced the idea of video as a social media tool. In his keynote at INBOUND 2016, HubSpot co-founder and CEO Brian Halligan described the current combination of social and video as the perfect marriage – like "scallops and bacon" to be precise – and that 50% of the content that marketing teams produce should be video.

The easiest ways to make your videos "share-friendly" include keeping your videos short, and making the content worth sharing! (Sounds simple enough!) To be more specific, social video — or "sharable" videos, are typically short, relevant, highly targeted, mobile-friendly, and often humorous. While funny videos are inherently more sharable, it's not always easy to produce funny videos! Don't force it, but do keep in mind the idea of making your video easy to share.

The more relevant, unique and compelling your video is, the more likely it is to be shared. Don't put any barriers in the way of getting your video passed along. If your video is too long, has poor production quality, or is simply not that relevant, it won't be shared (or even watched!)

However, if you remove any potential roadblocks to sharing, you've got a better shot at having your video liked, shared or retweeted. You can also make your videos easier to share by including share buttons with the video. This is an ideal strategy for video blog posts, where you control what the viewer sees. Adding social sharing buttons to a video blog post is a quick and easy way to encourage sharing.

Engage!

The other key to social video is to maximize *engagement* on your videos. You're putting your videos on social platforms, so you must be "sociable!" Engage, connect and interact with your viewers and encourage two-way communication.

Your video is not social until you've made some attempts at audience engagement. Thank your viewers for watching and sharing; respond to comments and keep the conversation going. The opposite of this engagement approach is what I call "post and ghost." Post and ghost is when you upload your video and then disappear. You become a ghost. You're talking at people, not with them. Don't post and ghost!

With the emergence of Facebook Live, Twitter Live and Instagram Live (and of course YouTube Live), you've got more opportunities than ever for engagement. These platforms are ideal for interaction because they're built for sharing and two way conversation.

Just consider the way users can tap their phones while watching your Twitter Live video to give you "hearts." Obviously, Facebook Live has a similar feature where viewers can "like" or comment in real time. Live videos provide the perfect opportunity for really involving your viewers and making your video really have an impact on your viewers and followers.

Keep in mind that video, and live video in particular, is all about connection, community and engagement. Much of that engagement will come after your video has been posted or after your live video has ended. So you can't simply "post and pray!" You've got to continue to respond to comments, interact and engage with your viewers long after your video makes its debut.

Keep the conversion going. Continue to build community around your video. And continue to share and distribute your video after the initial post. You should always encourage your viewers to share your video, as well.

Finally, video creators are often concerned that they're posting "too much," or that sharing the same video across several social media platforms is repetitive or redundant. Nonsense! You owe it to your viewers and potential customers to give them ample opportunities to discover your videos!

What if you only post your video to Facebook and many of your potential clients are not on Facebook (or don't see it the first time?) What if you Tweeted a link to your video, but 99% of your audience didn't see it in their Twitter stream? It's your job to get your video in front of as many eyeballs as possible, and that means sharing and distributing your video as proactively as possible!

What you may think as repetitive is actually the beginning of branding. Give your audience plenty of chances to see your video with consistent promotion and comprehensive distribution. More about repurposing and leverage in the next chapter...

CHAPTER 5 VIDEO KEYS

1. Get it off the hard drive! Your video (and all your effort) is wasted if the video never makes it off your computer or smart phone and on to platforms where it can be seen. Create a video distribution plan to ensure your video doesn't end up languishing on your hard drive!

2. Aim for the "I see you everywhere" effect! When you get your video off your hard drive and on to as many social media platforms as possible, you begin to achieve the "see you everywhere" effect. That means your videos are working for you, giving you visibility and exposure, 24/7.

3. Create a video promotion plan for increased "video visibility. As you plan where to post and distribute your video (i.e. your website, YouTube, Facebook, LinkedIn, etc), you're creating a powerful visibility strategy that's going to give you much needed exposure online. Be aggressive and don't hold back on your promoting your video!

4. Take advantage of "social video." So much of social media is being driven by video, so that gives you an opportunity to expand your reach and influence by posting your video across as many social media platforms as possible. When it comes to video visibility, more is more!

6

Video Power: Leveraging and Repurposing Your Videos for Increased Visibility

Closely related to Video Promotion is "Video Power." Video Power is really just a continuation and expansion of your video promotion, as it's where you leverage and repurpose your videos for maximum reach and maximum visibility.

As we alluded to in the previous chapter, some business owners are hesitant to promote their videos and share the same video across several platforms. If you're tentative about promoting and repurposing your videos, get over it!

At its core, video is a promotion and marketing tool, so never be shy about getting your video in front as many eyes as possible, as often and consistently as possible. You never know where that video view is going to come from — YouTube, Facebook, your website, LinkedIn, Instagram, etc — so leverage and distribute your videos as proactively as you can!

Whenever you think you're sharing or promoting your video too much, do more. You really have to be relentless when it comes to video promotion. There's so much noise and clutter online, that you have to rise above the chaos and make sure your video stands out in a crowded, hyper-competitive market.

I had a boss in the television business when I was in charge of marketing for a well known cable network, and he used to talk about

"2X4 Marketing." Naturally, I assumed this was some sort of special mathematical formula and fancy equation. Turns out that 2X4 marketing was a bit more literal: His interpretation of 2X4 marketing was that, the only way consumers would hear and remember your marketing message, would be to beat them over the head repeatedly with a 2X4 chunk of wood!

While you may not agree with the visual this suggests, I'm sure you get the point about the need to "hammer home" your message. I suggest you adopt (or adapt) this 2X4 "philosophy" when promoting your videos and beat your viewers over the head (figuratively, of course) with your videos!

Repurpose, Repurpose, Repurpose

You've no doubt heard the real estate refrain: Location, location, location. When it comes to video, the battle cry we use is: "Repurpose, repurpose, repurpose!" This means not only re-using and recycling your videos over time and across numerous platforms, but also repurposing your other digital assets that can be turned into video content!

Repurpose your existing blog posts, articles and ezines into videos. Repurpose longer videos into shorter versions. Repurpose webinars or tele-seminars into videos. Repurpose your live talks or speeches into videos. Repurpose your podcasts or slide presentations. You get the point. If you have any "digital assets" or intellectual property, you should be creating or re-creating it as video!

Remember the old expression "everything old is new again," and always strive to repurpose your content. You may very well be sitting on a goldmine of existing content that's just waiting to be turned into videos!

Again, don't think of it as "repetition;" think of it as branding! You want to give your fans and followers many chances and every opportunity to see your message., so you have to make it easy for your audience to find your content. Meet them where they're at! (Which is online!)

The other opportunity you have here is to integrate video into your existing marketing plans. Consider where video can not only supplement, but enhance, your current marketing efforts. If you're doing email marketing, try video email! If you're a blogger, mix it up with video blog posts. If you do podcasts, turn them into video podcasts.

Video Power!

The simple fact is that video can "power up" and boost all your existing marketing efforts. Video provides a true compounding effect that can exponentially increase your reach and influence. As such, you should carefully consider where and when you can use video to support and enhance your promotion plans, not just as another "thing" to do, but to improve your existing marketing plans.

Here are some practical applications of Video Power:

1. If you've got an "opt-in" page on your website to get visitors' email address (and you should), add an opt-in video that reiterates the benefits of signing up, along with a clear and compelling call to action. Using video on your opt-in or landing page can increase conversion rates by 80%. (according to Hubspot) With that type of impact, you'd be crazy not to include a video on your landing page!

2. The same goes for sales pages, where it is perhaps even more important and beneficial to include video. Not only can video on your sales web page make the page more engaging, but it's also going to put your sales page on steroids. After watching a video, 64% of viewers are more likely to buy your product online, while a whopping 90% of users say that product videos are helpful in the decision process.

3. Are you using email marketing? (Again, of course you should be!) Adding video to your email leads to a 200-300% increase in click-through rates. Depending on your email provider, integrating video with your email is relatively simple. You can embed a YouTube video, or add a photo or thumbnail that links to your video. (The user experience is the same. They click on the video or the photo and are taken to the video.)

4. Once you've got video in your email, be sure to include the word "VIDEO" in the subject line of your email, as simple adding the word video to the subject line increases your open rates by 19%, according to Syndacast.

5. If you're blogging, give you're blog a boost by switching up your written posts and adding a video blog post. They say a picture's worth a thousand words, but Dr. James McQuivey at Forrester Research has figured out that one minute of video is equal to 1.8 million words! Need more proof you should include video posts on your blog? Our friends at Wistia tell us that people spend 2.6X more time on pages with video than without.

6. In the previous chapter, we talked about the power of "social video." Adding videos to your Facebook page, or other social platforms, for that that matter, greatly increases your visibility. After all, over 8 billion videos (equalling 100 million hours of videos) are watched every day on Facebook, says TechCrunch. And a Facebook video receives 135% more organic reach than a Facebook photo. In fact, Facebook is rated as the most impactful social channel for video, at 8.4X higher than any other social channel, according to Animoto.

7. Perhaps the most compelling example of video power is live video — especially Facebook Live. We already know that people spend 3X more time watching a Facebook Live video than a video that's no longer live, but perhaps more telling is that Facebook users comment 10X more on live videos than they do on regular videos. Now that's engagement! And Twitter, another platform that has made it easy to go live, says that video of a live event increases brand favorability by an impressive 63%.

Even video ads are racking up incredible numbers: In a report from the Online Publishers Association, they state that 80% of Internet users recall watching a video ad on a website they visited in the past 30 days. On top of the remarkable recall numbers, 46% took some action after viewing the video ad, such as:

- 26% looked for more information about the subject of the video

- 22% visited the website named in the ad

- 15% visited the company represented in the video ad

- 12% purchased the specific product featured in the ad

The big takeaway on the dramatic power of video, according to Andrew Follett, founder and CEO at Video Brewery, is this: *"Video marketing increases sales and leads. If you're not a video marketer, you're losing customers to those who do. Businesses that incorporate video marketing into their overall marketing strategy see higher engagement rates, higher click-through rates and higher conversion rate. Why would you leave all that value sitting on the table?"*

The Wheel of Content

Think of your content or digital assets as your IP, or intellectual property. Your IP includes blog posts, articles, books, e-books, e-zines, presentations (slides), webinars, podcasts, social media content, and, of course, videos. Any content you've created can be repurposed or recycled for other platforms.

This is especially true of written content like blog posts or articles you've written. Most written content is ideal for repurposing as videos, because, in essence, you've already got your script! Consider starting with your written content, and then use what call the "wheel of content" to create a repurposing cycle.

For example, start with an existing blog post. (Make sure you've got an image that goes with the post). From your blog post, you can create an "image" post for Facebook with a link back to the blog. You can do the same with the image for Instagram and Pinterest. Once you've leveraged your visuals, you're ready to move on to repurposing the content as a video.

Use the same blog post as your script or outline for your video. You can deliver the content on camera, as a simple talking head video, or you can get creative and create a PowerPoint to video using slides.

(That PowerPoint can also be posted to slideshare.net as additional content!)

Whether your new video is on camera or off camera, you've now got a video "asset" that can be leveraged and spread across several platforms, from YouTube and Facebook, all the way back to your blog as a video blog post! The wheel of content cycle is now complete! Now simply "rinse and repeat" with additional content...

Your Leverage Ladder

Once you're cranking out new content and repurposing your videos, you can ascend the "leverage ladder" to continue to update and upgrade your content. You can use the Leverage Ladder worksheet below to jumpstart ideas for generating new content from your existing assets:

~~~~~~

LEVERAGE LADDER

Repurpose and recycle your products for maximum leverage and visibility...

- What content do you have that can be leveraged and repurposed? (Ebooks, articles, blog posts, tips?)

  _____

  _____

  _____

- What are your TOP 3 social media platforms that you use (or want to use?) Check all that apply:

  YouTube _____   Facebook _____   Twitter _____

  Google + _____   LinkedIn _____   Pinterest _____

  Instagram _____   Tumbler _____   Other   _____

- What are the biggest problems and challenges your clients face? (What are their Frequently Asked Questions?) This can be the basis for your tips series:

_____

_____

_____

- How will your repurpose your content for new platforms? (blog post to video, e-book to video, longer video to short video clips?) List your ideas here:

_____

_____

_____

The idea behind leveraging and repurposing is to integrate video into your existing marketing plans whenever possible, and create new and fresh content with video. What content do you currently have that can be repurposed as videos? Can you take written blog posts and "talk" them on camera to create video blog posts? Do you have podcasts that can be turned into video content? Get creative with your content so you're not constantly reinventing the wheel!

You should also determine how can video best support your marketing and promotion plans.

In many cases, you can use video to create far more effective and engaging sales pages, opt-in pages, blog posts, etc. Even if these web pages already exist, you can make them much more powerful (and increase your conversions), simply by adding video to the web pages.

A plain webinar registration page, for instance, can be much more personal and compelling with a video on the page, encouraging visitors to sign up for the webinar. The same can be said for opt-in or landing pages, where a video will enhance engagement and boost conversions. Even adding video to your "thank you" web pages can improve your viewer's experience — not to mention growing the all-important "know, like and trust" factor.

Consistency Counts!

The final ingredient for leverage and visibility is consistency. When it comes to video, I often warn that "one and done won't get it done!" Consistency is key for video visibility. When you put good content together with an ongoing and consistent video presence, you've got a recipe for marketing success!

With consistency, each video becomes another building block for your brand, and the cumulative result produces the "I see you everywhere" effect. Create a video editorial calendar or visibility plan to ensure that you're consistent and dependable with your video efforts. Here are a few tips for video consistency:

Being Consistent with Video Marketing

With so many on or off camera methods for creating video, you should no trouble do your first few videos. But video marketing, like any marketing, is not a one time event. Your video efforts need to be consistent and ongoing to get the most impact. Unless you want to succumb to the dreaded "one and done" syndrome, you'll want to create a strategic marketing plan for using video regularly in your business.

As with any plan, you must begin with the end in mind. What are your business objectives for video? Is it to grow your list? Build your brand? Drive more web traffic? Enhance your credibility? Your goals will determine your direction. If you said "all of the above" to the video goals we just listed, here are some ideas for maintaining your video momentum...

- **Create an "expert tips" series to share your expertise.** Short, 1 – 2 minute "how to" videos are a great way to increase your credibility and expand your influence. You can even record these all in one session, and then post your tips video to YouTube once or twice per week. A tips series provides some consistency and gives you added visibility on the web.

- **If you've got a blog, add a videoblog post every couple of weeks.** The search engines love video, and your readers will be treated to a dynamic change of pace from your traditional, written blog posts. Spice up your regular blog posts with video to make your blog more engaging. Extra bonus: Video is much more personal and compelling than print alone!

- **Get some face time.** Use a personal video message or video email to go "face to face" with your clients or prospects. Sending a video greeting, birthday wishes or a thank you video have much more impact than yet another regular email. Video email services like MailVu.com. and BombBomb.com make it point and click easy to record your video. If you want to stand out and be memorable, use video!

- **Make it an event.** Whether you're promoting a webinar or launching a new product, nothing makes a bold statement like video. Adding video to your promotional plans makes your webinar or launch look more like a special event. Again, it's the best way to break through the online clutter and make sure your message gets noticed.

- **Go Live!** You can do a live webcast or offer a "Q & A" video session using free platforms such as Facebook Live or BeLive.tv These web resources make it easy to fire up your webcam and go live whenever you want. A live webcast is dynamic, engaging and highly interactive. (You may want to do a test run first, just to get comfortable with the format).

However you decide to use video, it will put your marketing on overdrive and accelerate your results. The secret is consistency and strategy. Make a plan and stick to it. Anyone can make one video. The real winners online will be those who make online video a regular part of their marketing efforts.

Where and When

A key element to video consistency is knowing where and when to post. This will depend largely on your particular audience and niche, but there are some statistics that you can use as guidelines.

According to a study by Vidyard, the most popular viewing time for video is midweek and midday. More specifically, Wednesdays between 7 a.m. and 11 a.m. Pacific time. Tuesday and Thursdays are a close second, implying that the middle of the "work week" is prime time for video viewing. The Vidyard viewing times chart is below:

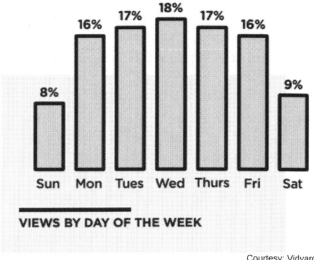

Courtesy: Vidyard

Just as important as when to post, is knowing where to post. Again, the Vidyard study comes in handy for determining your video distribution channels, as seen in the graphic below:

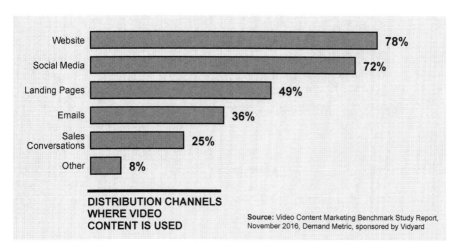

DISTRIBUTION CHANNELS WHERE VIDEO CONTENT IS USED

Source: Video Content Marketing Benchmark Study Report, November 2016, Demand Metric, sponsored by Vidyard

And finally, knowing the types of videos that businesses are investing in most will help guide your video strategy:

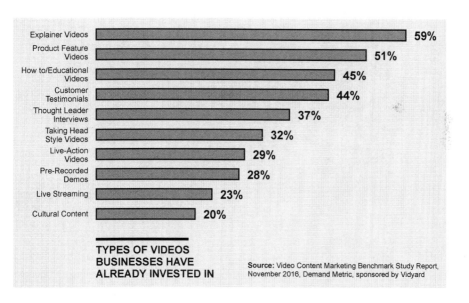

TYPES OF VIDEOS BUSINESSES HAVE ALREADY INVESTED IN

Source: Video Content Marketing Benchmark Study Report, November 2016, Demand Metric, sponsored by Vidyard

CHAPTER 6 KEYS:

1. Leveraging and repurposing your videos is the key to increasing
    your awareness and enhancing your video visibility. You need
    to be proactive and consistent when it comes to sharing,
    distributing and cross-posting your videos.

2. There's no such thing as "too much" promotion for your videos.
    Repetition and frequency are what will help your video stand out
    in a hyper-competitive marketplace.

3. You can exponentially increase the reach of your content
    by repurposing your existing assets (blog posts, articles,
    presentations, podcasts) into video content. Repurposing your
    intellectual property into videos will breathe new life into your
    "old" content.

4. Integrate video into your existing marketing plans. Consider
    where and when you can use video to support and enhance
    your promotion plans, not just as another "thing" to do, but to
    improve your existing marketing efforts.

5. Create a "wheel of content" to recycle your IP into different
    platforms, making it easy for your prospects to find your content.
    You can also use the "Leverage Ladder" worksheet to uncover
    and reinvent new assets that can be repurposed for video.

Video Profit: Monetizing Your Videos Through Product Creation and Sales

The seventh and final "pillar" of video marketing is really the Holy Grail of video: Monetization! This is where "sh*t gets real" and the rubber meets the proverbial road when it comes to success with video. The ultimate goal of any video is to make you more money. (Yes, your videos can serve or even save the world, but you're not saving anyone if you're broke!)

So in this very important chapter, we're going to show you how to monetize your videos and turn your video marketing into video profits! More specifically, we'll look at video content creation, as this is a cornerstone to monetizing your videos. We'll also explore video product and platform options, and touch upon webinar platforms and screencasting.

The three key steps to video monetization are:

1. **Develop and create your content:** This can be a video course, a video webinar, a membership program featuring video tutorials, individual video lessons or demos for sale, etc.

2. **Choose your delivery platform:** Once your video content has been created, you'll need to determine how you'll deliver or make available your content. You can make your videos available on your own website or via a membership platform such as thinkific.com,

or you can house your content on a third party site or software such as udemy.com or teachable.com.

3. **Determine your distribution methods:** You will also need to decide how the content itself will be created and disseminated. Will you need webinar software to create your video lessons, or will you require special web pages or landing pages? This is the "nuts and bolts" of video course creation.

Logistics aside, there are essentially two ways to make money from your videos:

First, you can create videos that promote and market your products and services. I would argue that every video you create, either directly or indirectly, exists to build and promote your business. 99% of the videos you create will subtly or overtly "sell" you and your services. Video is first and foremost a sales tool.

Second, the video itself can be a product to be sold. You can create video products to sell, whether they be a video series, video tutorials, event videos, webinar videos, a video course, etc. Your video products for sale can be a physical product like a DVD, or a digital product online.

In the first case, where you're monetizing by using your videos as a promotion and sales tool, there are any number of directions you can take: Obviously, you can create promotional videos that directly market your products and services. Think of these as your "TV ad" or traditional advertising or commercial videos.

You can also create a series of "product launch" videos to build buzz and excitement for your new products you're launching. This tried and true method of pre-promoting your products typically features content rich "teaching" videos, designed to add value and create awareness in advance of a new product launch.

In addition, you can create content marketing videos for your information products, or promotional videos such as live event videos, interview videos, or even "video summits" featuring a series of video interviews.

Creating videos to drive webinar or event registrations is another example of using video as a sales and marketing tool, as is creating speaker "sizzle" reels or portfolio videos to show off your work. Business owners often create sizzle or promo videos to generate visibility, awareness and "buzz" for their live events.

Of course, a standard sales video or "video sales letter" (VSL) has become a staple in the world of online marketing. A video on a sales page can make the sales message much more compelling. The sales video can simply be an element on the sales page but, in same cases, the video is the sales page. Many business owners have found success using the sales video as the primary aspect of the web page.

In summary, you can make money from your videos through:

- Video Information Products

- Video Webinars (for free or for fee!)

- Video Product Launch

- Video Content Distribution (Udemy)

- Video Events (Live Webcasts)

- Video Membership Sites

Video Product Creation

Creating and selling video products is a powerful and popular way to profit from your videos. There are a host of excellent reasons for creating video products, not the least of which is that it's simply the way the world is moving! Most consumers prefer video products and would rather watch than read -possibly because we're a society raised on television and visual mediums.

In addition, video products have more potential for repurposing and repackaging: Several video tutorials can become a video course or online workshop, for example. Video webinars can also be repackaged and sold, as can videos of live events or presentations.

Video products often provide a much better user experience, and thus more customer satisfaction. Because there is a higher perceived value with video products, you can usually charge more for video products than you could for the same content delivered as an e-book or audio recording.

Finally, creating and selling video products provides you with more opportunities for strategic alliances and joint ventures, as most partners will assign a higher value to products delivered via video. That's why developing video products allow you to play at a whole new level!

Perhaps the most compelling argument for creating video products is that your video courses, workshops or tutorials become evergreen products that generate passive income. By selling your video products, you're creating recurring revenue that does not require your direct time. Having video products to sell gets you out of the "trading time for dollars" trap and allows you to scale your business more quickly. You create your product once and sell over and over again!

Video product creation also provides you with tremendous flexibility. There are numerous ways to create your video product:

You can do a virtual class or workshop delivered via video lessons; you can create video webinars, either for a fee, or free with an upsell to another product or service. You can produce video summits or conduct a guest interview series as a video product. Or you can do video webcasts and charge admission. Other options include putting together a video product launch or develop a membership site where content is delivered via video.

When it comes to building your video product and deciding exactly what to create, you should first consider what type of video product will best support your business objectives. You may also want to think about any "holes" in your product funnel, in terms of price points. Maybe you already have a low barrier to entry $27 product, and a higher ticket $997 product, but nothing in between. That could be an opportunity to develop a $397 or $597 video product to give you a mid-range priced product.

Keeping your business goals in mind as you plan and develop your video product will also help you determine your platform, whether it's strictly educational, or if it's promotional. You can also take your live event and use the video recordings to create a video product. Aside from the platform, you'll also want to decide on the price point of your product, and whether or not your video product will be a digital download or a physical product like a DVD.

Here's a brief "product checklist" you can reference when planning your video product. Be sure to ask yourself these questions to gain clarity and direction

- Is it marketable?

- Will it sell?

- Does it fit into your overall business strategy?

- Does it fill a need in your target market?

- Does it fill a hole in your product funnel?

- Do you have the time and resources to create it?

If you're not sure, one easy way to decide is to simply survey your fans or followers. Use the poll function on Facebook, or utilize software such as SurveyMonkey to create a quick poll for your peeps!

Another handy "mini-tool" for developing your video product is to refer to this Content Planner and ask the following questions:

- What content do you have that could be repurposed for video content?

- What type of video product or products do you want to create?

- What type of video product would best support your business objectives?

- What resources or materials do you need to produce your video product?

- How will you market, sell and deliver your video product?

As we've said before (and it bears repeating), any intellectual property you create can be turned into a video product that you can offer for sale!

1. Your recorded webinar becomes a video product

2. Your live event becomes a video product

3. Your signature speech becomes a product

4. Your articles or lessons become video products

5. Your audio interviews become products

One of the benefits of creating video products is that there are so many ways to deliver your video content. There are all kinds of options for "slicing and dicing" your video products, whether you want to produce online video tutorials, create more traditional recorded video webinars, produce a video interview or "summit," or do a livestream video or webcast.

As many methods as there are to produce your video content, there are just as many ways to "deliver" it, or decide where the video product actually "lives." You can, of course, house the content on your own website or blog — or you can put up a "pay wall" and password protect your video content if it's for sale only.

You may prefer to host or store your content on a third party video hosting site, such as Wistia or Amazon S3. Other delivery methods include a private membership website, or perhaps even "old school" physical DVDs.

Creating Your Video Product

Now that you've seen the potential for video products, it's time to reveal the real "nuts and bolts" of putting your video product together! Just like with video, your video product development should begin with the end in mind. What is the purpose of your product? Your goals will again help dictate what type of video product to create.

Let's make the safe assumption that the goal of your video product is revenue generation. You want a product that you can sell over and over again to create recurring revenue that does not require your one on one time. One key objective of having a video product is getting you out of the "trading time for dollars" trap.

With that in mind, let's create a 4-module video course, or online workshop, that you can sell for $397. Your pricing will depend largely on your niche and your audience, so you'll have to make the determination on what to charge. However, for online video products, my own personal rule of thumb is typically to charge about $100 per module — assuming each module or recording is like a webinar that's about 45 minutes to an hour long. So another way to look at it is to charge $100 per hour of content.

Now that we've decided on our format (4-part video course) and our pricing, we get into "production" mode: You're creating a video product, so you'll have to determine how you want to present your content via video. Do you want to be on camera, presenting as you would in a live environment? (If so, you could simply videotape your live presentation.) Or do you prefer to share your content off-camera, such as by narrating a PowerPoint presentation or recording a screencast? (You can also create a hybrid combination of on and off camera for variety/)

I prefer (and recommend) a mostly off-camera approach, as most audiences don't want to watch a talking head for an hour — and you may not prefer to be on camera all that time. Remember, in this example, we're creating a 4-module, or 4-part video course, where each of the modules is like a separate, 45-minute webinar. With that in mind, a narrated PowerPoint presentation is often your best bet for delivery.

PowerPoint (or screen capture) is my "go to" format, but I usually appear live on camera for the beginning and end of each section. This provides some "connecting" time and the opportunity to add your own personality to the presentation. Using a platform like zoom.us (more on that soon), you can toggle back and forth between appearing on camera and sharing your screen.

Now we have to actually create the content that will be shared on video. You'll have to draft or outline how you want to present each section. Again, my default is to create a PowerPoint presentation that serves as both an outline and a graphic visualization of the content — making it easy for viewers to follow along as I narrate my content.

Insider Tip: Make your presentation as visually compelling and attractive as possible, as this is the "look" of your product. Boring black and white text won't cut it. Forget the usual "death by PowerPoint" presentations that typically dominate, and get creative and colorful. Of course, you'll want to stay "on brand" with your presentation — but that doesn't mean bland! I find gorgeous PowerPoint (or Keynote for the Mac) templates at GraphicRiver.net. GraphicRiver is a marketplace for graphics and presentation templates. You can find affordable and professionally designed themes that you can use as your presentation template.

Once you've decided on a template, you can build your presentation and add your slides with your content. Follow the usual best practices for presentation creation and keep your slides clean, uncluttered and not over-crowded with text. Use visuals and images whenever possible.

When your presentation "deck" is complete, you're ready to record your video! There are any number of ways to record your presentation, but I prefer a "webinar-style" format using a screen recording software such as Zoom. Again, I prefer zoom.us because it's affordable, user-friendly, and very flexible. Zoom gives me the ability to share my screen and either switch back and forth between on camera or screen share, or share my screen and stay on camera in an inset on screen. Please note that you can actually record on Zoom for up to 40 minutes for free.

You can also record with or without viewers. For a clean, controlled recording, you can simply record on Zoom with no audience, and just narrate the slides as you scroll through the presentation. *Another Insider Tip!* I often deliver my online workshop live the first time through, and the recordings of the webinars become my recorded product! That way, I can sell my live class, and create my recordings at the same time.

Getting back to our video product example, you have now created your 4 modules, or 4 separate PowerPoint presentations, and you can record each either live or without an audience. When I do my live online workshops, I typically deliver one class or webinar per week for 4 weeks. Record your content as you see fit, and do any minor edits to make sure you've got a clean recording.

Next, you'll decide where you want your content to "live," and how your buyers will access it. You'll want to use a delivery platform that doesn't require a lot of manual work for you, so find a "hosting" solution that's as automated as possible. You can house your video recordings on your own website (perhaps behind a paywall), or use membership software, such as Wishlist Member. I use (and recommend) Thinkific, a robust, yet easy to use membership platform.

Thinkific allows you to upload and organize your videos, PDFs, audios, documents, or any other course materials. You can also add quizzes and monitor your students' progress as they work through your course. The paid versions of Thinkific also integrate e-commerce, so you can sell your courses right through the platform. Paid plans start at $39 per month.

One of the reasons I'm a big fan of Thinkific is that, once your customer purchases your course, you can simply send them a link to Thinkific where they can access the content. The student can then watch the videos or download the PDFs on their own, and at their own pace. The process is automated, so I can sell courses in my sleep!

You can set up the pricing and e-commerce elements inside Thinkific, or you can use another system for the sales piece (I use Infusionsoft), and simply integrate the two. In my case, I create a sales page connected to my shopping cart, and when the buyer makes the purchase, they're automatically sent an email with the access link for the video course. Obviously, there's some set up and administrative tasks involved, but once the tools are integrated it's pretty much "set it and forget it!"

With your content created, recorded and hosted, all that's left is the crucial sales and marketing piece. Once you've got a way to "deliver" your course, i.e. Thinkific, you've still got to sell it!Again, for the email marketing and e-commerce aspects, I use Infusionsoft; but there are dozens of platforms or plugins you can use as your "shopping cart" to sell your courses.

You'll also need a sales page or video sales letter to promote and sell your video course. Once again, there are many options online for creating sales websites or pages — but I use LeadPages. I love LeadPages because they've got hundreds of templates or sample web pages to choose from. Once you find your template, you just replace the copy and graphics with your own.

LeadPages makes it super simple to create your own sales pages, and it integrates with your shopping cart so your customers can simply click on the "buy" button and be taken to a checkout page. LeadPages also has designs for "thank you" pages, so once your customer buys, they're take directly to a thank you page.

Many LeadPages and now "drag and drop" making them even more flexible and customizable. And most LeadPages include a section for video, so you can add your own sales video to your sales page. You can get your own LeadPages account using my link at: http://www.leadpagesrocks.com/

To summarize the video product creation process, you can follow these steps:

1. Decide on your format — Do you want to create a 4-part video course, a 10-day video challenge, or a mini-course with short, 10-minute video tutorials.

2. Set your pricing — What you charge is up to you, but will depend on your target market and your particular niche.

3. Determine your delivery method — What tools will you use to record your videos? You can set up your recording like a traditional webinar using webinar software, such as WebinarJam or WebinarNinja, or you can use a screen recording tool like zoom.us or GoToWebinar.

4. Pick your platform — Next, decide whether you want to deliver your content on camera, via screencast, or some combination of both. I recommend that you create a

PowerPoint presentation that you can then narrate over the slides.

5. Find a hosting solution — Your content (videos) will need to "live" somewhere, so figure out where you will host or house your videos. I use thinkific.com as my "membership" site.

6. Set up your e-commerce — You'll also need a shopping cart to handle the e-commerce side of your course. You can also use a simple solution such as PayPal or Stripe.

7. Market and promote your course — You can sell your video course via a sales page, using web page creation software such as LeadPages.com

Before we wrap up this section on video monetization, let's take a closer look at some of the key tools you can use to create and market your video products: Since we're producing video products, you'll need to determine the most appropriate tools for actually recording your videos.

We've already discussed using PowerPoint or Keynote to create the visuals or "slides" for your video presentation. If you'd like to spice up your PowerPoint, check out PresenterMedia.com, where you can add animated elements to your presentation. However, you're not limited to PowerPoint. You can also use software such as prezi.com to make your presentations more animated and dynamic.

If you're using screencasts to create your video product, you'll likely want to explore Techsmith's line of screen capture software, most notably, Camtasia. Techsmith also offers more affordable screen-casting solutions, such as SnagIt and Jing. If you're on a Mac, you might prefer Screenflow.

For the actual recording of your video content, you can go with zoom.us, or the more expensive GoToWebinar. Another, more 'end to end,' option is WebinarJam. WebinarJam is a complete marketing solution that provides webinar registration pages, thank you pages, the "event" page, and replay pages. In addition to making it easy to set up the webinar web pages, WebinarJam also offers marketing tools in the form of confirmation and reminder emails sent from the system, making it a great 'one-stop' solution for your video webinars — from registration to replay!

When WebinarJam first launched, the webinars (events) were held on Google Hangouts. However, they recently created their own platform called "JamSession." This is a more stable platform that provides you with more control, so you're no longer dependent on Hangouts. Best of all, the new JamSession technology now streams directly to YouTube Live. (You can set the privacy settings if you don't want to make the YouTube video public.)

One other resource that's crucial for selling and marketing your video product is your sales page. This is where you list your video product for sale and tout the benefits of your product. This page will have a "buy" button that links to your shopping cart so customers can purchase your product online, anytime, 24/7.

There are many options and tools for creating your sales page, including simply creating a new page on your own website. However, I use and recommend the previously mentioned LeadPages, since this is often the quickest and most effective way to create a professional sales page (or any kind of web page for that matter!)

With software like LeadPages, you can create a stand-alone web page specifically for promoting and selling your video product. LeadPages has hundreds of pre-designed page templates, so all you need to do is choose a template and customize it with your own information. The simplicity of LeadPages means you can build your sales page quickly and easily, without waiting for your web designer or tech support person. LeadPages takes the guess work out of creating your sales pages, since all the elements — headlines, videos, social proof, etc — are already built into the templates. (See sample pages below) I use LeadPages nearly every day and could not run my business without it. Again, you can explore what they have to offer at: http://www.leadpagesrocks.com/

Finally, when your video product is complete and you've created a sales page to sell it, you can expand your sales and distribution platforms by exploring third-party sites to sell your product or course.

We've already mentioned Thinkific, which is a great option for hosting and selling your video courses.

In addition to Thinkific, there are a number of third-party websites and platforms where you can upload and sell your products. Perhaps the best known is Udemy, which now offers over 45,000 courses. You can post your video course on Udemy and take advantage of the huge, built-in audience on their marketplace. Of course, Udemy keeps 50% of the proceeds, but you can't beat the potential exposure.

I've got several video courses on Udemy, including one with over 5,000 students from 139 countries! Visit udemy.com for details and check out the screen shots here:

Other online platforms for uploading and distributing your video course or product include Teachable, Skillshare, Ruzuku, and the very popular lynda.com. If you've yet to develop a large following, these online marketplaces can be a great way to get your video products out there!

CHAPTER 7 VIDEO KEYS

1. Monetizing your videos can come in the form of using your videos to promote your products and services, or from using the videos themselves as products to sell.

2. The three key steps to video monetization are: Develop and create your content; choose your delivery platform; and determine your distribution methods.

3. You can make money from your videos through Video Information Products; Video Webinars; Video Product Launches; Video Content Distribution (i.e. Udemy); Video Events (Live Webcasts); or Video Membership Sites.

4. The process of video product creation can be broken down into the following steps: Decide on your format; Set your pricing; Determine your delivery method; Pick your platform; Find a hosting solution; and finally, Market and promote your course.

5. Some of the tools and resources you may want to consider to assist in your product creation and marketing include: thinkific.

com for hosting and distributing your content; zoom.us or
WebinarJam.com for recording your videos; LeadPages.net for
creating your sales pages to sell your video course or product;
and udemy.com for selling and distributing your courses.

So that's a wrap on Part 1, the Seven Stages of Video Marketing. You
can refer to the infographic below and use it as your "Video Marketing
Road Map" to video marketing domination!

Here's a quick review of what we've covered so far:

Stage 1: **Video Purpose:** Establishing Your Video Goals and Objectives

Stage 2: **Video Premise:** Developing Your Video Content and Messaging

Stage 3: **Video Production:** Determining Your Equipment and Technical Needs

Stage 4: **Video Platforms:** Finding Your Video Sweet Spot and Style

Stage 5: **Video Promotion:** Sharing and Distributing Your Videos for Maximum Reach

Stage 6: **Video Power:** Leveraging and Repurposing Your Videos for Increased Visibility

Stage 7: **Video Profit:** Monetizing Your Videos Through Product Creation and Sales

PART 2

The Practical Guide to
Making Great Videos

8

How to Get Started with Video

This section and following chapters are designed to be a reference guide for getting started with video, and will also demonstrate not just how to produce videos, but how to produce *great* videos that actually accomplish your business objectives!

Always keep in mind that the goal is not just to "make a video." Video is a marketing tool — a means to an end. Anyone can bang out a video. The real genius comes in creating a video that "moves the dial" and gets you closer to your overall business goals. Think in terms of what you want your video to accomplish. What action do you want your video viewers to take?

Before we get started, we have to address why you may not have started! What's been holding you back? If we get those "excuses" out in the open and address the most common roadblocks, you can face your video fears and dive in. Let's dig deeper and address the excuses we hear most often:

5 Lame Excuses Why You're Not Doing Videos (and How to Start!)

At this point, you may feel like they've the Online Video Revolution without you. The train has left the station. You're yesterday's news. Use whatever cliché you want, but the hype is true. The Internet is being driven by video. In fact, 90 percent of all Internet traffic will be video within the next few years, according to Cisco and YouTube.

Simply put, if you're not embracing video, you're missing a huge opportunity.

So why are you still putting it off? Here are the five most common lame excuses, along with some tough love suggestions for getting your video act together:

1. You don't like the way you look on camera

Are you camera-shy or just plain uncomfortable on camera? Join the club. For the vast majority of us not blessed with George Clooney or Jennifer Aniston good looks, being on camera is not a natural, everyday thing. That leaves you with two options:

Plan A is to suck it up, buttercup! Get used to it. Practice. Work at it. Force yourself outside your comfort zone until it gets easier. (Otherwise, you can do what I do and hide behind kids, costumes, pets or props!)

If you're absolutely dead set against being on camera, or you've got a pimple the size of Cleveland on your forehead, then you've got to go to Plan B: Skip the camera altogether and do a PowerPoint video, screencast, photo montage, or some other "off-camera" alternative. We've given you dozens of off-camera ideas in earlier chapters.

2. You're technophobic

If you can do PowerPoint, you can do video. If you have a webcam, you can do video. If you have Facebook, you can do video. Heck, if you have an iPhone, you can do video! Video has become mainstream, low-tech and easier than ever. The truth is you need very little equipment or technical skills to crank out decent video. Fear of technology is no excuse, because today there's so little technology required to produce video.

3. You don't have time

Make time. Video marketing is an investment and you'll find that it's time well spent. Your first few attempts may take a little more time, but once you develop a process that works for you, you'll get better and faster at it. Stick to your system and the time challenge won't be as daunting as you think. I set aside a few hours on the weekend and "batch" record several videos at the same time. The time commitment is not nearly as bad as you imagine.

4. You think it's too expensive

This is old-school thinking. Sure, it used to be cost-prohibitive, but you're not making a major motion picture or producing a Superbowl commercial. YouTube is free; Facebook is free; webcams are $30 dollars... You can even edit your video right on YouTube for free. And if you have a smart phone, you have a video camera in your pocket. Even if you really want to go hog wild and get studio lights or editing software, you don't need to spend more than a couple of hundred bucks. Start where you're at, with what you've already got!

5. You're not sure where to begin

Steven Covey said it best: "Begin with the end in mind." Where you begin depends on where you want to go. Think about your goals for your video. What's your business objective? More visibility? More leads? Better search engine optimization? Do you want to be the next viral sensation or do you just want a video on your home page to introduce your business to your web visitors? Your goals will drive your video strategy, so begin at the beginning!

So there you have it. Excuses eliminated. Problems solved. Now go forth and make video! The sooner you add online video to your marketing mix, the better and stronger your business will be.

If you're still in a state of overwhelm, know that you're not alone. Anything new can be a bit intimidating, and making videos clearly falls outside most of our comfort zones. You may have to stretch a bit to tackle this new, but very rewarding, phenomenon called video.

In over ten years of working with entrepreneurs and small business owners on video marketing, I've heard every excuse in the book, and we've been able to overcome every obstacle. Yet, in all that time, the same three, major challenges seem to come up, again and again.

In the early days, the biggest stumbling block was technology. That was a legitimate concern "back in the day," but those days are over. Now, there's little, if any, tech needed to create great videos. The truth about tech is that trial and error is the best teacher.

Another common challenge is simply fear of being on camera and being afraid that you'll somehow make an ass of yourself on video. Again, this fear is mostly unfounded, but certainly understandable. If the previous chapters have taught you anything, I hope that it's that video doesn't need to be scary.

The third and final most common video complaint is that it just takes too long. "I don't have time" is a common refrain we hear when we encourage our peers and followers to tackle video. Marketing with video not only offers a significant return on investment, but it also produces an excellent and worthwhile "return on time." Every video you create is like your own, personal "marketing clone" that's out there working for you!

Still feel like video will take too much time? Here are five shortcuts that will help you save time (and reduce stress) when it comes to creating your videos:

Five Time-Saving Shortcuts for Creating Kick-Ass Videos

I talk to scores of well-intentioned entrepreneurs who realize they *should* definitely be doing more marketing videos for their businesses but, as the saying goes, the path to Hell is paved with good intentions.

Intending to produce more business videos and actually creating those videos is NOT the same thing. And, as we've seen, the culprit is usually time — the great equalizer.

Making game-changing videos can be time-consuming initially, but there are several strategies that can help you work smarter, not longer. Based on my experience writing and producing hundreds of videos, here are my tried and true time-saving tips:

1. Focus on Goals Over Gadgets

The biggest mistake — and often the biggest time-suck — is getting caught up in video gadgets and the latest bright, shiny objects. *"What camera should I use?"* is not the question you should be asking! What is the goal of your video, and what's the best way or the best tool to achieve that objective?

I've seen too many video newbies spending countless hours trying to figure out some groovy new software, when they could have created the same video using a much simpler tool they've already mastered. Use the right tool for the job — and use the easiest tool whenever possible!

2. Know Your Why Before You Fly

Closely related to the first tip above, you've got to know *why* you're creating your video in the first place — before you dive in! If an ounce of prevention is worth a pound of cure, then an hour of prep time can save you hours once you start taping.

It's called "pre-production" for a reason. Adequate planning and preparation before your fire up the webcam or press record will save you hours of frustration once you move into the production phase. Have a road map for video creation and follow it!

3. Find Your Video Sweet Spot

Another notorious time thief is when we get bogged down doing the "wrong" type of video. I help my clients find their video "sweet spot," meaning the appropriate video platform for their specific goals and their personality.

Most people "default" to on-camera, talking head videos. But their "sweet spot," may be another type of video altogether — like animation, or a narrated PowerPoint video. When you create the best kind of video for you, video marketing becomes a lot easier — and a lot faster!

4. Tame Your Technology

Even if you must venture outside your "sweet spot," you should still commit to simplicity. Don't make your project any more complicated than it needs to be. Avoid the temptation to use a fancy, super-techie video camera when an iPhone or iPad will do just fine. We tend to want to make video much harder than it has to be. The KISS rule applies here!

5. Done is Better Than Perfect

Finally, you've got to know when it let it go! Perfection is the enemy of the good, and never has that been more true than with online video. Obviously, we want to produce quality video and put our best face forward. But at some point, you've got to yell "Cut! That's a wrap," and send your video out into the world. Never let your video languish on your hard drive because it isn't absolutely perfect. Get it done and get it out!

Video has become a powerful and pervasive marketing tool, and it's quickly becoming a "must have" for your marketing mix. Fortunately, the tips above will take the "overwhelm" out of video and help you create great videos more quickly and easily then ever before.

While we're on the subject of "video fears," here's one more quick list of ideas for overcoming what I call "Video Performance Anxiety." VPA can strike at any moment and can even afflict seasoned video veterans. Video Performance Anxiety is like a last minute "crisis of confidence" that usually strikes just before you're about to record your video. Fortunately, it's mostly a "mind over matter" issue that can be conquered with the right attitude.

With that in mind, here are ten quick tips on how to be cool on camera:

Overcoming "Video Performance Anxiety" – 10 Ways to Be Cool on Camera

One of the biggest fears most entrepreneurs have about using online video to market their business is *not* about technology or how to create the video. If you're like most small business owners, the biggest fear you face is that you'll make an ass of yourself on video. You're afraid you'll look like a fool or a fake. Or you're worried that people will criticize your video or – even worse – simply ignore it.

I've given this common syndrome a name: VPA, or *Video Performance Anxiety.*

VPA is widespread among small business owners. Most entrepreneurs would rather have a root canal than appear on camera. Fortunately, there are many ways to overcome Video Performance Anxiety and actually look cool on camera. Maybe not George Clooney cool, but cool enough for your colleagues and prospects to respect you and want to work with you.

I've come up with a list of 10 different ways to be cool on video – Each of which should give you the confidence to go forth and share your message with the masses. Pick one or more of these tactics and fire up that webcam!

Be relevant – Be topical. Be timely. Share content that will resonate with your target market. Talk or teach about something that will strike a chord with your viewers.

Be funny – Humor is not easy, but it's very effective. If you can pull off funny, go for it. Funny videos are the most popular and most shared videos you can create. Give it a shot. The payoff can be enormous!

Be engaging – You can talk *at* people, or you can talk *with* them. Think of your video as a conversion. Engage your audience. Reach out to them. Encourage feedback. Ask for a response. And be sure to include a call to action in all your videos.

Be real – Be yourself. Be authentic. Don't imitate, innovate! The real deal will always play better than BS. Keep it real!

Be bold – Say what you think. Arouse controversy. Don't be afraid to piss some people off. Express yourself fully. Take chances!

Be different – If everyone zigs, it's time to zag! Lead, don't follow. Experiment and explore. It's okay to "go rogue" on your video. Different gets noticed. Different is good.

Be your brand – Think of each video as a building block in your branding. Use your video soapbox to develop and expand your brand. Be consistent and focused. Stay on topic and stay on message.

Be generous – Share your content generously and frequently. Give 'til it hurts, then give some more. Video is the perfect tool to share your gifts and spread the love! Provide value and be a giver before you promote.

Be moving – Emotion connects, and real emotion connects big time. If you can use your video to move and inspire your viewers, you'll be more than just cool on camera – You'll be loved!

Be money – Better yet, show your tribe how to make money! Use your video platform to show your audience how to be successful. Show *them* the money!

If you can run with even one of these 10 ways to be cool on camera, you'll never again suffer the embarrassment of Video Performance Anxiety. Together, we can beat VPA forever!

The bottom line is that getting started with online video is the same as getting started with anything. You just have to start at the beginning or, as Stephen Covey once said, "The main thing is to keep the main thing the main thing."

Do plan, but don't overthink. Starting your video marketing efforts really can be as simple as firing up your computer's webcam or hitting record on your smart phone. Keep you key business goals in mind, and then decide the quickest video route from point A to point B. Don't make it any more complicated than it needs to be. Remember, the better your planning, the better your video!

With that in mind, let's review the planning process and give you a step by step process for getting started...

How to Create a Video Plan That Works

As we've discussed, the biggest challenge with online video is just getting started. For many entrepreneurs, even those who have no problem cranking out content, creating video content can be daunting and intimidating.

And once you've got that first momentous video finished, you've only just begun. "One and done" does not work when it comes to video marketing, so you need a process and you need a plan!

The key to a successful, ongoing video marketing strategy is to develop a video plan that supports your overall business objectives. In fact, it's not enough to just "do video," you've got to create videos as a means to an end. Your videos should be designed to help achieve specific business goals.

What do you want your video to accomplish? Are you doing video for the visibility and exposure? Are you trying to build credibility and establish yourself as an expert in your niche? Do you want to improve your search engine rankings? Or perhaps you're looking to video as a way to generate leads and sales for your business. Your goals will determine your video direction.

Planning is the key to video marketing success.

Be sure to set realistic goals that support your business. Specific video goals may include:

- Developing a video presence online

- Adding an opt-in or welcome video to home page

- Creating a "video tips" series on YouTube to establish credibility and expert status

- Building a promotional platform to sell books or information products

- Creating a sales video to launch a product

- Starting a weekly videoblog series to consistently deliver your content

- Creating tutorials or demos to sell as video product

Try not to think of video as an "add on" or an extra thing you have to do. Video can be integrated into your current marketing plans. Make a list of your regular marketing activities (i.e. email marketing, blogging, social media) and decide how adding video can enhance or improve those marketing tools.

That may mean turning blog posts into video blogs, doing a video version of your ezine, or just adding video to your email marketing efforts by sending video mail. (Two services for easy video mail include Bombbomb.com and MailVu.com).

Once you've set your goals and determined how to integrate video into your existing marketing plans, you can get more specific by scheduling your video activities using a video editorial calendar.

A Video Editorial Calendar can help you plan and organize your video schedule.

A video editorial calendar will help keep you on track and ahead of the curve when it comes to producing your videos. If you know, for instance, that you've got a new product launch or a big webinar to promote in March, you can work backwards and determine when you'll need to shoot and produce a promo video.

Now that you've got all your ducks in a row with planning and scheduling, you just need to refine your video process. Obviously, the process will vary depending on the type of video you are producing, such as on-camera or off-camera. Either way, you've got to create a step-by-step system that you're comfortable with — and one that can be easily repeated as needed.

If you're doing a typical on camera "talking head" video, your process might consist of:

1. Scripting — Having an outline or script so you're ready with what to say

2. Appearance — Are you ready for your close-up?

3. Staging and setting — Finding an appropriate spot where you can shoot your video

4. Lighting — Making sure you've got adequate light

5. Audio — Testing your sound to ensure good audio quality

6. Camera — Testing your webcam or video camera to make sure the shot looks good

7. Recording — Getting the right take that you're happy with

8. Editing — Making edits and embellishments as needed

Again, your process can be as simple and streamlined as you want to make it. As long as it works for you, and you can repeat the process whenever you want, you'll be good to go!

As you can see, the best videos are actually created before your ever fire up the webcam. Planning your video is the key to a successful shoot. Taking the time to plan ahead will make it much easier to create your videos — and to crank out quality videos consistently!

How to Make Your First Videos

Let's get down to "brass tacks." I'm not sure where that expression came from, but we have reached the point in this book where "the rubber meets the road," we get the ball rolling, and we "get jiggy with it!" In other words, t's time to actually make a video...

Let's take a look at the step-by-step process of video creation in the real world, both for on-camera videos and off-camera videos. We'll start with the tried and true talking head video:

On-Camera Videos

As you know by now, "talking head" videos are often the "default" video mode, so it's important to know how and when to use this method. Most often, your typical "head and shoulders" video is going to be shot with your webcam, or possibly with your smartphone or tablet. This is arguably the most common type of video, and has been a staple since the beginning of television.

When to use:

On-camera videos should be used when you want to convey a direct message or appeal to your audience, which is why they're often used for sales videos, web home page videos, and many other marketing messages.

Your talking head video can be as simple as talking directly to the camera, or as complex as a fully edited video with all the editing bells and whistles you wish to add. At it's core, it's you talking to the camera as if you were talking to a friend or colleague or prospect. Common uses include:

- Home page video
- About me video
- Sales video
- Personal "explainer" video
- Event or webinar invitation video
- Thank you for buying video
- State of the company video, etc.
- Interview video

Keep in mind that most live videos or webcasts, such as Facebook Live, are talking head videos, as well. The same holds true for Instagram videos or Twitter Live videos, though you'll be using your mobile device as the camera for those platforms.

What you'll need:
Again, this type of video can be as simple as hitting record on your smart phone or webcam. You'll essentially just need a camera for recording, which will likely be the webcam that you use on your desktop or laptop computer.

You could just as easily use your iPhone, iPad, or any other smartphone that includes video recording capability. If you're using an older, more traditional video camera or camcorder, you'll have to go through the extra step of getting the footage off of that camera and into your computer to edit or upload. We recommend simplicity whenever possible, so use your your webcam if you can!

What it costs:
If you've already got a webcam on your computer or laptop, you're good to go! Similarly, if you have a smartphone or tablet, such as an iPhone or iPad, you're also ready to record.

If you're starting from the very beginning, then get yourself a webcam that can be connected to your computer or laptop via USB. Logitech webcams are always a safe bet, and run anywhere from $30 to $130.

The Logitech HD Pro Webcam C920 is a bestseller at about $60.

Overcoming Deer in the Headlights Syndrome: 3 Quick Tips for Not Freezing Up On Camera

They say fear of speaking in public is right up there with fear of death. Yikes! If that's true, then speaking on camera must also be one of the biggest and most universal fears. There may not be a room full of people when you're shooting your marketing video, but the minute that camera goes on, many of us go into a state of mild panic.

If you'd rather run for cover than be on camera, you're not alone. It's natural to be self-conscious when you need to be in front of the camera. Even seasoned professionals still get a bit of stage fright. Back in the day when I was at E! Entertainment TV shooting television commercials and celebrity interviews, we'd actually turn off the "tally" light on the camera – it's the little red light that indicates "recording." We'd disarm the tally light just so the interview subject would be less nervous. Eventually, after a few takes, the person on camera would relax and focus on their message, instead of worrying about the camera.

That's just one of the keys to better on-camera video: Focus on your message. The more you concentrate on delivering your content and engaging your audience, the less aware you'll be that there's a camera there. Stay "on message," just as political advisors would recommend to their candidates.

Here are three more tips for looking like a pro when the cameras roll:

Rehearse, rehearse, rehearse.

Television and movie celebrities practice and rehearse relentlessly, and so should you. Take a cue from Hollywood and be prepared. Review your script up and down and sideways before you ever fire up your video camera.

Plan it. Script it. Shoot it.

You've got to have a strategy and a well-thought-out plan for every video you create. If you want to look comfortable on camera, then you need the confidence that a real strategy provides. Plan your video shoot in advance. Understand your objectives and what the video has to do to accomplish those objectives. Then script it out. It doesn't have to be word for word, but it you do need to organize your thoughts and – at the very least – have a detailed outline for what you're going to say. Only then are you ready to shoot your video.

Suck it up, buttercup!

Finally, if you still feel like a deer in the headlights when the camera rolls, just deal with it! (Insert tough love here!) Seriously, you may have to get outside your comfort zone to be on camera, but the end result is well worth it. The more you do it, the easier it will become. You will make mistakes at first, but that's what re-takes are for! If Hollywood can do 27 takes of one scene, so can you! You've got to start somewhere, so just start!

For more video marketing tools, tips and resources, please visit http://www.loubortone.com.

Off-Camera Videos

The possibilities for off-camera videos are almost endless. There are dozens of options and a wide range of tools and apps for creating video that doesn't require you to be on camera. Off-camera videos include animation, PowerPoint, "sketch" videos, explainer videos, screencasts or screen capture videos, "kinetic" text videos, motion graphics, and the list goes on and on...

When to use:

You can use off-camera videos for just about any purpose or occasion. As is always the case, it depends primarily on the goals for your video. "Explainer" videos are a popular off-camera option, often used to demonstrate or explain how a product or service works. Animated white board or "sketch" videos are another popular option, as are cartoon-style animated videos. Screencasts are also quite common, and PowerPoint slides to video is becoming more mainstream, as well.

The short answer for when to use this style of video is simply whenever an off-camera method will be more powerful or engaging than a "talking head." Of course, there are many business owners who loathe the idea of being on camera, so off camera videos can be a viable alternative if you're dead set on avoiding the spotlight.

Off-camera videos are also ideal for longer videos, presentations, demos, or webinars that require more than the usual 2-3 minute video. I create all my webinars in PowerPoint, then use zoom.us to narrate and present the information on screen. Sales videos, or video sales letters, are also used often as an alternative to the traditional talking head video. You can convey a lot more information and keep your viewer's attention with text, animation and motion. Again, you're really only limited by your imagination.

What you'll need:

Simply put, what you'll need is the Internet! Or more specifically, a working knowledge of the vast options available to you when it comes to video websites, apps and software. While we reviewed many of these tools in earlier chapters, here's an overview of the easiest resources for getting started:

PowerPoint to Video — Create your presentation in PowerPoint (or Keynote on the Mac), and record your video either right within the software, or with a screen capture program such as Camtasia, Zoom, or Screenflow if you're on a Mac.

What it costs: Nothing if you've already got PowerPoint, plus the cost of Camtasia or Screenflow if you go that route. I'd recommend using Zoom to keep the cost down.

Photo Montage Videos — Video montages are a very quick and simple way to produce off camera videos. You can use photos, text, and even video clips to create a professional-looking video that won't break the bank. My two "go to" resources for photo montage videos are animoto.com and stupeflix.com.

What it costs: Animoto has a 14-day free trial, then plans begin at $8.00 per month. All plans

Explainer or Animated Videos — You can use animation software such as VideoMaker FX, websites such as Powtoon, GoAnimate, Animatron, Magisto, Videoscribe, Moovly, or any of the new sites which seem to pop up almost daily. Most of these tools offer free trials, so testing and experimenting is recommended for discovery which one is the best solution for you.

What it costs:

- **VideoMaker FX** — http://www.loubortone.com/videomaker — $47 – $67 lifetime, depending on if they're running a promotion or sale

- **Powtoon** — https://www.powtoon.com/ — Free to start. Premium plans start at $19 per month

- **GoAnimate** — https://goanimate.com/ — 14-day free trial, then plans start at $39 per month

- **Animatron** — https://www.animatron.com/studio/ — Free to try; $15 – $30 per month, depending on the plan.

- **Magisto** — https://www.magisto.com/ — Plans start at just $9.99 per month (paid annually)

- **Videoscribe** — http://www.videoscribe.co/ — $12 per month (paid annually)

- **Moovly** — https://www.moovly.com/ — Plans start at just $5 per month

Hybrid Videos

If you prefer to do some combination of talking head, on-camera video and screen capture or off-camera video, then there are several methods for creating "hybrid" videos.

When to use:

A hybrid video with both on and off camera elements can be the best of both worlds, so there are plenty of opportunities to use this format. One that comes to mind as extremely useful is a video webinar, where you can appear on camera to welcome your guests, then switch over to screen sharing to show your slides, then switch back to on-camera to make an offer or close out your webinar. The ability to "toggle" back and forth between on camera and screen sharing is ideal for webinars and live video presentations.

You can also use this "toggle" method if you're doing a video tips series: You simply start on camera to establish rapport and build trust; then switch to your slide or graphic while sharing your tip; then reappear on camera at the end for a call to action or close.

The same goes for any kind of video tutorial, demo or course you may be creating. Starting out on camera gives the viewer a chance to establish a connection with you, and makes the video more personal and engaging. But sharing a lot of information is often better as a presentation, so the off-camera, or screen sharing piece is equally important. If you're doing video tutorials, you can again come back on camera to re-establish the connection with your audience.

What you'll need:

There are several tools which allow you to toggle back and forth between on camera and screen sharing. Some, like Camtasia and Go To Webinar, give you the option of staying on screen as an "inset," or picture in picture, while you present your slides.

I prefer and recommend Zoom (zoom.us), which is a simple and affordable web conferencing option. Zoom is easy to use for both the user and the viewer, and it allows you to bounce back and forth from being on camera to sharing your screen. I use this for all my video webinars, as well as for creating video tips and tutorials. Zoom provides both MP4 recordings and MP3 audio recordings of your presentations.

What it costs:

- **Zoom** — The free version of Zoom allows you to host up to 100 participants for up to 40 minutes. If you're video presentations or webinars go over 40 minutes, you'll need a paid version of Zoom, which starts at just $14.99 per month.

- **Go To Webinar** — The much pricier Go To Meeting/Go To Webinar software may be more feature rich, but it comes at a premium. After the 7-day free trial, Go To Webinar plans start at $89 per month for 100 participants. If you go over 100 participants, you need to bump up to the hefty $199 per month plan, which allows up to 500 participants.

Live Videos

Finally, there's the increasingly popular live video format. In some respects, this is the absolute easiest way to get started making videos, as it's really as simple as a few taps on your iPhone. Early adopters of live video, or live streaming, had to use Periscope, or the short-lived Blab. But Facebook Live took live video to the masses, and made live streaming much more mainstream.

When to use:

The ease and accessibility of live video means that you can "go live" anytime, anywhere. Live streaming is perfect for any on-the-go, in-the-moment activity, whether you're on a walk with the dog, or at a live event. Live videos can be planned or spontaneous, at home or on the road (no, not while driving), or alone or in a group setting. Live video is also ideal for "quick" (as opposed to "keeper") videos, whether you're checking in from an event or trade show, or doing a spur-of-the-moment video rant or editorial. Live is the ultimate "anything goes" video.

What you'll need:

The beauty of live video is that it was mostly designed for mobile devices, so your smart phone or tablet is a great place to start. You'll need a mobile app such as Periscope or, more likely, Facebook, to go live, but that's essentially it!

What it costs:

Nada! Most mainstream live video platforms, such as Facebook Live and YouTube Live, are free, making them easily accessible to everyone with an Internet connection and a smart phone. Even third-party apps like BeLive.tv and Smiletime, which enhance and expand your live video capabilities, are free (at the moment).

So there's really no excuse not to go live, especially since live video has become the "low hanging fruit" of video marketing. With a few taps on your smartphone, you can begin "doing video" and sharing your message with the world.

Whether you choose to do live video, pre-recorded on-camera videos, or some off-camera method, the important thing is to start and, once you've started, to be consistent. This is why I talk so much about finding your video "sweet spot." Once you discover your most natural video style and format, chances are good that you'll make video a habit. And that "video habit" is the secret sauce that will grow your business exponentially!

Video Tips, Tricks and Shortcuts

By now, you should have everything you need — information, resources, tools, and know how — to create great video. From here on, it's a simply a matter of reaching into your new bag of video tricks and pulling out what you need to achieve your marketing objectives.

So I've reserved this final chapter to share my favorite video "hacks," or shortcuts, to help you streamline the video process and crank out videos faster and with more ease. What follows is a collection of tips, tricks and tools for making video a breeze!

My Favorite Video Hacks!
7 Simple Video Shortcuts to 10X Your Video Productivity
Video marketing can be incredibly effective for entrepreneurs and small business owners who

- need to compete with bigger, better funded competitors. Promoting your business with video

- can level the playing field and give you a huge advantage because video builds the "know, like

- and trust" factor and accelerates the sales process.

However, many entrepreneurs feel that video marketing is beyond their reach because it can be so time consuming and complicated. Many people are missing out on the online video revolution because they fear the time commitment of doing video.

Fortunately, video does not have to take a ton of time or effort. There are all kinds of shortcuts and hacks for making video simple. Here are my 7 favorite video productivity tips:

1. **That Jing Thing**

Go download Jing at https://www.techsmith.com/jing.html. (Free) This simple sibling of Camtasia is more than a screen capture tool. You can also instantly record your screen for up to 5 minutes. It's perfect for quick screencast videos or mini-slide shows. Just fire it up and start talking over your computer screen. Best of all: The 5 minute limit keeps you focused and succinct... a must for videos!

2. **Zoom in on video**

If you prefer to be on camera, or if you want the flexibility of being able to toggle between on camera and screen sharing, then zoom.us is the perfect solution. Zoom offers video conferencing and online meetings, but more important, video recording. (Free for up to 40 minutes; Pro Plans start at $14.99/month). You can host up to 50 participants on the free plan, but the real "hack" here is to use it as a video recording tool. Record yourself or your screen (even with no participants), and you've got a fast and easy video!

3. **Go Live**

Facebook Live, Periscope and now, Instagram and Twitter, all give you the ability to broadcast live with just your smartphone. With just a couple of taps on your phone, this may be the quickest and easiest way to create a video. And because platforms like Facebook Live are designed to be recorded "in the moment" and on the fly, there's no need nor expectation for fancy editing or post production. Just hit record and go!

4. **Montage Mania**

Having a bad hair day or don't want to appear on camera? Then simply pull together a few photos and create a quick photo/video montage. Low and no cost tools like stupeflix.com, animoto.com, and Adobe Spark for the iPad (https://spark.adobe.com/) make it super simple to upload images or graphics and add words and music to create a great video.

These services even provide stock photos, themes and free music to go along with your montage.

5. Vmail is the new Email

Video email is far more engaging and effective than traditional email, because you get to connect directly with your viewer in a much more personal way. Vmail is perfect for direct outreach or follow up after a meeting or event, and it's as simple as talking into your webcam or smartphone.

Video email services like bombbomb.com start at $39.99 per month and offer custom branding, email templates and more.

6. PowerPoint to Video

Whether you're using PowerPoint on a PC, or Screenflow on a Mac, you can narrate and record your slide presentation and save it as a video. This is a great way to repurpose your existing assets if you have any PowerPoint presentations, and it's also the ideal way to conduct webinars.

7. Tube Tips

You can record directly to YouTube, or use YouTube Live, to record a quick video tips series. Even if you're just using YouTube Live as a recording platform with no audience, the "hack" here is that your recording goes directly to your YouTube Channel.

Cranking out great video doesn't have to be a chore. Use any of these time-saving video hacks and watch your video productivity soar!

Sweet Shortcuts

When all is said and done, the best video hack, and the single most effective shortcut, is simply finding your video "sweet spot," and using your favorite video method as your go-to process. We talked a lot about discovering your sweet spot, but it bears repeating.

Once you find the right style of video that's a fit for you, you can create video much more quickly and effectively. An even greater benefit is that you might just enjoy it! If video making becomes fun for you, you'll do it more often and get better results!

So while there are plenty of tools for making video simple, the very best shortcut is just a matter of using your ideal form of video. For me, it's video powerpoint, which I can use anytime to record video tutorials or present online video webinars. I'm comfortable with the format, my fans and followers enjoy it, and it's relatively easy for me to create.

For you, your sweet spot may be simple "talking head" videos, Facebook Live broadcasts, explainer videos, or some other style. The only real way to know is to try several methods and see what feels best. It's a decision based mostly on personal preference, but at least partly on what you need to accomplish with video. As always, your goals will help determine your direction.

Aside from the "golden rule" of finding your video sweet spot, other video shortcuts or hacks can be as simple as finding a go-to recording tool, like zoom.us. While Zoom is primarily a video conferencing software, it's screen-sharing and on-camera capabilities make it the perfect device for recording your videos — with or without an audience.

I use Zoom as a video recording device because it quickly and cleanly gives me an MP4 video file that's ready to edit or upload. Incidentally, Zoom also provides an MP3 audio file of your recording, should you need it for a podcast or other audio use.

Other new recording tools seem to be released almost weekly, so there are always new options for creating video. A few of my newer favorites are Loom, (www.useloom.com), Vidyard's "ViewedIt" (https://viewedit.com/) and Wistia's "Soapbox." (https://wistia.com/soapbox).

All three are similar in that they are all Google Chrome extensions, and all three allow you to instantly record your screen and/or your camera from your desktop. While Loom is my personal favorite, ViewedIt and Soapbox serve essentially the same function. These new tools make recording a video just as fast (if not faster) than typing an email, so they're perfect for sending video emails.

Email is a hack unto itself, as it can be a powerful and personal way for direct outreach. (Just check your in box to see how many emails you've received today, versus how many video emails!) You can use Loom, ViewedIt or Soapbox to crank out quick, simple and engaging videos that have way more impact than standard email.

Videos by the Batch

Another video "hack" that I use and recommend for my students is to "batch" your videos. This is simply a matter of doing a bunch of videos at once. It's especially efficient for on camera or talking head videos. As long as you're all "dolled up" to appear on camera, and you've got your lights and setting in place, why not record a bunch of videos at the same time?

While this requires some planning and preparation, "batching" can be extremely productive and rewarding. I batch shoot my videos whenever I'm doing a tips series or a collection of video tutorials. I create my topics and outlines in advance, then just record one video after another.

It's also helpful to carve out time and actually "schedule" your video creation into your calendar. Blocking off a chunk of time and devoting it to shooting your videos takes some of the pressure off and helps ensure that you'll actually get it done. (It's like writing your goals down!) I typically set aside a few hours on a Sunday afternoon if I know it's going to be relatively quiet.

The batch method is a great way to prioritize and "calendarize" your video production. While you can never completely control your environment, try to find a time when the kids aren't home and there are no distractions, and allow yourself enough time and space to focus solely on video.

Don't Overthink It

Finally, the last secret to streamlining and simplifying video is to not overthink it! We tend to want to overcomplicate the video creation process. We worry, we procrastinate, and we dally. We end up making it a much bigger deal than it has to be. Keep things simple. Don't overthink. Plan, yes — but don't obsess over it! Just jump in and find the shortest distance between you and a finished video. It doesn't have to be so hard!

Of course, confidence only comes with practice and preparation. And confidence is half the battle. Tackle your video projects head on and with the same tenacity and persistence you'd give to any other worthwhile endeavor. Action cures fear. Just get started.

You got this. And I've got your back. Always.

Bonus Materials

Lou Bortone's
Video Marketing Programs and Courses

Find all Lou's video classes at
http://www.loubortone.com/classes

Video Marketing Success System ($397) — Lou's "master class" for online video marketing. 6 video modules, plus worksheets, PDF guides, etc.

14-Day YouTube Challenge ($97) — Become a YouTube marketing expert in just 14 days! 19 short videos, 3 PDFs.

7-Day Facebook Live Video Challenge ($97) — Become a livestreaming video pro in just 7 days! 12 videos, 5 PDFs

Video Script Templates Bundle ($97) — 20+ "fill-in-the-blank" video scripts, plus video training and bonuses.

Video Production Blueprint ($97) — Everything you need to know to produce your videos. 6 videos, 4 PDFs.

Video Kickstart Kit ($97) — How to create your customized video marketing plan. 4 videos, 11 PDFs.

Video Essentials Bundle ($97) — 10 Essential Video Tutorials, including "how-to" videos, video tips, and bonus video webinars. 20 videos, 10 PDFs.

Online Video Secrets, Shortcuts & Hacks! ($97) Special collection of video tutorials, checklists, worksheets and PDF guides.

Video Checklist Bundle ($97) — The ultimate video marketing resource. 6 videos, 26 PDFs!

Video Marketing Shortcuts ($27) — How to get started with video marketing quickly and easily. 7 videos, 4 PDFs

Video Editing Mini-Course ($27) — Video editing tutorial. 1 video, 2 PDFs.

Lou Bortone's
Video Tools and Resources

*Video Equipment

Blue Snowball Mic — http://www.loubortone.com/blue

Green Screen set-up — http://www.loubortone.com/greenscreen

Lighting Kit — http://www.loubortone.com/lights

*Video Creation (VideoMaker FX, etc)

VideoMakerFX— http://www.loubortone.com/videomaker

VideoScribe — http://www.loubortone.com/sketch

*Video Web Pages & Website Creation (LeadPages)

LeadPages — http://www.loubortone.com/leadpages

*Video Webinars (WebinarJam)

WebinarJam — http://www.loubortone.com/webinarjam

*Video Freebies

25 Best Video Tips — http://www.loubortone.com/tips

5 Favorite Video Tools — https://loubortone.leadpages.net/5faves/

Easy Video Studio Guide — https://loubortone.leadpages.net/resource-guide/

http://www.loubortone.com/lous-tools-best-video-marketing-resources

Note: I am an affiliate for several of these resources, so I may get a small commission on any purchases. I never promote nor endorse a product or service unless I test and use it myself.

Video Content Planner

Turn your existing "information assets" into video products...

1. What content do you have that could be repurposed for video content?

   _____

   _____

   _____

2. What type of video product or products do you want to create?

   _____

   _____

   _____

3. What type of video product would best support your business objectives?

   _____

   _____

   _____

4. What resources or materials do you need to produce your video product?

   _____

   _____

   _____

5. How will you market, sell and deliver your video product?

   _____

   _____

   _____

Video Script Templates

Use these templates as a starting point for your video scripts and just fill in the blanks!

Always remember our AIDA formula when scripting: Attention — Interest — Desire — Action

- What are you going to talk about/Why should they listen

- Who you are and who you serve (target market)

- What you can do for them — What's the result you get?

- Why they want what you can provide — Ultimate benefit

- Small taste or sample of the value you provide

- Call to Action — What should they do next?

- Give the viewer specific directions for the next step

WELCOME/HOME PAGE VIDEO

IF YOU'RE LOOKING FOR (product or service you provide), THEN YOU'RE IN THE RIGHT PLACE! WELCOME TO (name of company or site). I'M (your name, duh), AND I'M GOING TO (show/tell/explain to) YOU HOW WE CAN HELP YOU (receive/get/have) (the big benefit, result or outcome your product/service provides).

IF YOU'RE SICK AND TIRED OF (key problem or pain point your target market has), THEN WE'VE GOT A GREAT SOLUTION FOR YOU! IN FACT, WE'VE HELPED (dozens, hundreds, thousands) OF PEOPLE (or occupation) JUST

LIKE YOU GET RID OF (key problem/pain point) ONCE AND FOR ALL! HOW DO WE CONQUER (problem)?

FIRST, WE (solution #1 that you provide). THEN, WE (solution #2). FINALLY, WE (solution #3 — try to give an example or case study to drive the point home).

SO IF YOU'D LIKE TO TAKE THE FIRST STEP TO (solve problem your product or service provides), THEN YOU CAN GET STARTED BY DOWNLOADING OUR FREE (free sample or product you offer, i.e. e-book, special report, video tutorial). JUST ENTER YOUR NAME AND EMAIL ADDRESS IN THE SPACE BELOW, AND YOU'LL RECEIVE IMMEDIATE ACCESS TO OUR (freebie/download offer). OF COURSE, IF YOU HAVE ANY QUESTIONS OR WOULD LIKE TO GET IN TOUCH, YOU CAN (CALL OR) EMAIL US ANYTIME AT (your email address or contact info). BE SURE TO CLICK THE LINK BELOW, AND WE'LL SEE YOU ON THE NEXT PAGE... THANKS!

WELCOME VIDEO ALTERNATE

WELCOME TO (your company name)! WE'RE A (type of company or product) FOR (market you serve/target market). WE'RE UNIQUE/DIFFERENT IN THE (industry niche) BECAUSE WE (unique selling proposition or point of differentiation). WE MAKE IT EASY FOR YOU TO (achieve/get/have the end result client wants). IN FACT, YOU CAN (achieve outcome) BY SIMPLY (using the method/system your company provides). (Your system/solution) IS THE FASTEST (OR EASIEST) WAY TO (reach desired outcome) EVEN IF YOU STRUGGLE WITH (challenge #1) OR (challenge #2). WITH (your company name), IT'S NEVER BEEN EASIER. WE'RE KNOWN FOR (unique feature or value proposition of your company). SO WHAT ARE YOU WAITING FOR? (Call to action) GIVE US A CALL/SIGN UP BELOW AND (your company) WILL (help achieve customer's goal). (Add company tagline if appropriate).

ABOUT ME VIDEO

Note: Unlike your welcome video, which should focus on your target market's problem, your About Me video is an opportunity to provide more background on your skills and experience, and on why YOU are the best choice for your prospects. You should provide additional details about yourself or your company, but all of the details should support the argument that the best thing for them is YOU!

HI, I'M (your name), AND I'M SO GLAD YOU'VE VISITED THIS PAGE... I WANTED TO TAKE A MOMENT TO TELL YOU A LITTLE BIT MORE ABOUT MY BACKGROUND AND EXPERIENCE, AND WHAT THAT MEANS TO YOU... I HELP (your target market) DO/GET/HAVE/ FIND (solution your provide and key benefit your product or service achieves) SO THEY CAN (ultimate result your target market wants!) MY ____YEARS EXPERIENCE WITH (companies you've worked for, experience or jobs that make you qualified) MAKES ME UNIQUELY QUALIFIED TO (solve the problem, get the desired outcome, etc). I'VE

HAD THE OPPORTUNITY TO WORK WITH (name companies, brands or people you've worked with successfully). (Optional: YOU CAN SEE WHAT THEY'VE SAID ABOUT US ON OUR TESTIMONIALS PAGE).

WHEN I WAS WITH (former job or position you held), I WAS ABLE TO (or I WAS PART OF A TEAM THAT) (List the key accomplishmentS or success stories that relate to your target audience and the goal they are trying to achieve.) MORE RECENTLY, I'M PROUD TO SAY THAT I (list a recent goal achieved for a client, or a key accomplishment — it's okay to brag here a bit!) I'D WELCOME THE OPPORTUNITY TO GET THE SAME KIND OF RESULTS FOR YOU! IF YOU'D LIKE TO LEARN MORE ABOUT ME AND HOW I CAN HELP YOUR BUSINESS, PLEASE CALL OR EMAIL ME AT (contact info) OR CLICK ON THE LINK BELOW TO DOWNLOAD OUR (free offer). I LOOK FORWARD TO CONNECTING WITH YOU SOON!

ABOUT ME SAMPLE

HI, I'M LOU BORTONE, AND THANKS SO MUCH FOR VISITING THIS PAGE... I WANTED TO TAKE A MOMENT TO TELL YOU A LITTLE BIT MORE ABOUT MY BACKGROUND AND EXPERIENCE, AND WHAT THAT MEANS TO YOU... I HELP SMALL BUSINESS OWNERS JUST LIKE YOU GET MORE VISIBILITY WITH VIDEO, SO THEY CAN ATTRACT MORE CLIENTS AND INCREASE THEIR REVENUE. MY 20 YEARS EXPERIENCE WITH MAJOR NATIONAL BRANDS LIKE NBC, E! ENTERTAINMENT TELEVISION AND

FOX MAKES ME UNIQUELY QUALIFIED TO HELP YOU WITH YOUR MARKETING CHALLENGES AND PUT YOU ON THE MAP. AS SENIOR VICE PRESIDENT OF MARKETING FOR FOX FAMILY WORLDWIDE IN LOS ANGELES, I HAD THE OPPORTUNITY TO LAUNCH TV SHOWS, BRANDS, AND EVEN ENTIRE CABLE NETWORKS. MORE RECENTLY, I'VE HAD THE OPPORTUNITY TO WORK WITH BESTSELLING AUTHORS AND SPEAKERS LIKE MICHAEL PORT, MSNBC'S CAROL ROTH, FACEBOOK EXPERT MARI SMITH, AND DOZENS OF OTHER THOUGHT LEADERS. YOU CAN SEE WHAT THEY'VE SAID ABOUT US ON OUR TES- TIMONIALS PAGE. WHEN I WAS WITH E! IN HOLLYWOOD, I WAS PART OF A TEAM THAT GREW THE CABLE NETWORK TO NATIONAL PROMINENCE. MORE RECENTLY, I'M PROUD TO SAY THAT I'VE HELPED NEWBIES AND ESTABLISHED EXPERTS AS WELL RAMP UP THEIR VIDEO MARKETING EFFORTS TO GET THEM NATIONAL EXPOSURE AND MORE REVENUE. I'D WEL- COME THE OPPORTUNITY TO GET THE SAME KIND OF RESULTS FOR YOU! IF YOU'D LIKE TO LEARN MORE ABOUT ME AND HOW I CAN HELP YOUR BUSINESS, PLEASE CALL OR EMAIL ME AT VIP@LOUBORTONE.COM OR CLICK ON THE LINK BELOW TO DOWNLOAD MY FREE "5 MUST HAVE VIDEOS" GUIDE. I LOOK FORWARD TO CONNECTING WITH YOU SOON!

THANK YOU PAGE VIDEO

Note: This one can be short and sweet. You simply want to acknowledge the action your viewer took, whether it was to download a free offer, register for a webinar or purchase a product...

CONGRATULATIONS, AND THANK YOU FOR (downloading our freebie, purchasing our product, etc) (Tell the viewer exactly what happens next, i.e.) WATCH YOUR EMAIL FOR INSTRUCTIONS ON (using the product or freebie, etc) AND BE SURE TO WHITELIST OUR EMAIL ADDRESS SO YOU RECEIVE EVERYTHING YOU'VE REQUESTED. I KNOW YOU'RE GOING TO LOVE (product or service they requested or purchased). IF YOU HAVE ANY QUESTIONS OR NEED ANY HELP, BE SURE TO EMAIL US AT (contact info or support desk email). THANKS AGAIN, AND WE LOOK FORWARD TO ASSISTING YOU!

Optional: Some Thank-You pages feature an additional offer or upset, so be sure to include the "Call To Action" in your thank-you video! Your thank you page can also include a request to share your info with social media, so add those "share" buttons as appropriate, and ask the viewer to share!

YOUTUBE CHANNEL TRAILER VIDEO

NOTE: Your YouTube Channel Trailer is essentially your "welcome" video for your YouTube Channel. This video can be similar to your home page video, but with a different call to action at the end.

HI, THIS IS (your name)... WELCOME TO MY YOUTUBE CHANNEL, AND THANKS SO MUCH FOR VISITING! ON THIS CHANNEL, YOU CAN FIND (list the types of videos you post and how it can help or benefit your target market)! PLEASE FEEL FREE TO CLICK AROUND AND CHECK OUT (direct them to a specific video or playlist).

MY VIDEOS ARE (add another brief description of the your best videos and what's in it for the viewer). SO I HOPE YOU'LL SUBSCRIBE TO MY CHANNEL SO YOU CAN STAY IN THE LOOP AND LEARN MORE ABOUT (subject you cover in your videos).

ONE MORE THING! MAKE SURE YOU VISIT MY WEBSITE AT (your web address) WHERE YOU CAN FIND (freebie or irresistible offer). SEE YOU SOON!

YOUTUBE TIPS VIDEO INTRO/OUTRO

Note: A video Tips series on YouTube can be very powerful, and can get you a great deal of visibility quickly. "How to" videos are extremely popular on YouTube, and you can take advantage of that by sharing your knowledge and expertise..

Intro:

HI, THIS IS (your name) FROM (your company or website). I HELP (your target market) GET/DO/ACHIEVE (main result or outcome you get for your target) SO THEY CAN (key benefit or benefits your clients enjoy from your result). IN THIS (3-part, 4 video, 5 day, etc. — Give the viewer a sense of how many videos in the series) VIDEO SERIES, I'M GOING TO (show you/ demonstrate/teach you) HOW TO (what you're teaching/ sharing and the big result it leads to). (Offer proof that you're the right person to share this info) I'VE BEEN (teaching, studying, working) (target market)

HOW TO (what you do/teach) FOR OVER (X years). (You can also mention clients or companies you've worked with as additional social proof).

NOW I WANT TO SHARE THAT (knowledge/expertise/secrets) WITH YOU... (SHARE YOUR TIPS/CONTENT HERE — BE SPECIFIC AND/OR OFFER CASE STUDIES OR SUCCESS STORIES)

Outro:

BE SURE TO WATCH FOR THE NEXT VIDEO IN THIS SERIES, WHERE WE SHARE (preview subject of next video in series). (Include your call to action here!) FOR MORE DETAILS ABOUT (your area of expertise) JUST VISIT/CALL/SIGN UP AT (your website or sales page) WHERE YOU CAN (offer or benefit they can get) AND GET RESULTS EVEN FASTER! I LOOK FORWARD TO SEEING YOU ON THE NEXT VIDEO...

(If this is the final video in the series, adjust the ending to reiterate and emphasize your call to action or what you want the viewer to do next!)

WEBINAR INVITATION VIDEO

HI , IT'S (your name) WITH A QUICK/IMPORTANT MESSAGE FOR (target market)... IF YOU'RE STRUGGLING WITH (key problem or pain point of target market that's addressed in your webinar), THEN YOU'LL WANT TO SAVE THE DATE AND SIGN UP FOR (name of webinar), COMING UP ON (webinar date and time). DURING THIS CONTENT-RICH, NO FLUFF LIVE TRAINING, WE'RE GOING TO SHOW YOU/REVEAL

- Key share/benefit #1
- Key share/benefit #2
- Key share/benefit #3

WHEN YOU JOIN US ON THIS LIVE TRAINING, YOU'RE GOING TO WALK AWAY WITH (ultimate solution or outcome your information will provide)... IF YOU CAN'T MAKE THE DATE, BE SURE TO SIGN UP ANYWAY SO YOU CAN GET FREE ACCESS TO THE RECORDING. BUT DO TRY TO JOIN US LIVE, SO YOU CAN GET YOUR QUESTIONS ANSWERED LIVE RIGHT ON THE WEBINAR! SO REGISTER TODAY AND JOIN US ON (date/time) FOR (repeat name of webinar — It should ideally include the "promise" of the webinar). SIGN UP NOW AND WE'LL SEE YOU ON THE WEBINAR!

WEBINAR INVITATION VIDEO SAMPLE

HI, IT'S LOU BORTONE WITH A QUICK MESSAGE FOR SMALL BUSINESS OWNERS WHO WANT MORE VISIBILITY AND MORE CLIENTS... IF YOU'RE STRUGGLING WITH CREATING GREAT VIDEO, THEN YOU'LL WANT TO SAVE THE DATE AND SIGN UP FOR 'SUPER SIMPLE VIDEO MARKETING' COMING UP ON MAY 25TH AT 2PM EASTERN. DURING THIS CONTENT-RICH, NO FLUFF LIVE TRAINING, WE'RE GOING TO SHOW YOU:

* HOW TO RAMP UP YOUR VIDEO EFFORTS QUICKLY, EVEN IF YOU'VE NEVER DONE VIDEO BEFORE

* THE SIMPLE VIDEO TRICK THAT WILL HAVE YOU CREATING GREAT VIDEO TODAY

* THE 3 'VIDEO KILLER' MISTAKES THAT YOU ABSOLUTELY MUST AVOID... AND MUCH MORE!

WHEN YOU JOIN US ON THIS LIVE TRAINING, YOU'RE GOING TO WALK AWAY WITH THE CLARITY AND CONFIDENCE TO TACKLE ONLINE VIDEO FOR YOUR BUSINESS, SO YOU CAN GET THE VISIBILITY AND RECOGNITION YOU DESERVE! IF YOU CAN'T MAKE THE DATE, BE SURE TO SIGN UP ANYWAY SO YOU CAN GET FREE ACCESS TO THE RECORDING. BUT DO TRY TO JOIN US LIVE, SO YOU CAN GET YOUR QUESTIONS ANSWERED LIVE RIGHT ON THE WEBINAR! SO REGISTER TODAY AND JOIN US ON THURSDAY, MAY 25TH FOR "SUPER SIMPLE VIDEO MARKETING!" SIGN UP NOW AND WE'LL SEE YOU ON THE WEBINAR!

WEBINAR THANK YOU VIDEO

NOTE: Use this video on your Thank-You page to welcome and reassure your prospect who has just signed up for your webinar. You also have the option to leave out the date, and make this a "generic" thank you for signing up video...

THANKS FOR SIGNING UP FOR OUR WEBINAR! I KNOW IT'S GOING TO BE WORTH YOUR VALUABLE TIME, BECAUSE WE'LL BE SHARING (key webinar benefit or solution you'll reveal)! SO WRITE DOWN THE DATE AND TIME, AND JOIN US LIVE ON (webinar date). YOU CAN ALSO BOOKMARK OR PRINT THIS PAGE, SO YOU'LL HAVE ALL THE DETAILS READY FOR THE TRAINING. IN THE MEANTIME, KEEP AN EYE OUT FOR OUR REMINDER EMAILS, AND SHOOT US AN EMAIL AT (your email address) IF YOU HAVE ANY QUESTIONS. WE LOOK FORWARD TO SEEING YOU ON THE TRAINING!

ABOUT THE AUTHOR

"Sweet Lou" Bortone is known as The Video Godfather. We're not exactly sure why and, frankly, we're a little afraid to ask. What we do know is that Lou Bortone has been a pioneer and thought leader in the video space since the launch of YouTube in 2005. He's helped thousands of entrepreneurs and companies create and leverage online video to build their brands and dramatically grow their revenues.

Prior to his industry leading work in online video marketing, Lou spent over 20 years as a marketing executive in the television and entertainment industries, including stints as National Promotion Manager for E! Entertainment Television and Senior Vice President of Marketing for Fox Family Worldwide in Los Angeles.

Lou is a popular speaker, author, and ghostwriter of six business books. You can learn more about "Sweet Lou" at LouBortone.com.

Made in the USA
Columbia, SC
12 November 2018